AMERICAN POETS PROJECT

AMERICAN POETS PROJECT

IS PUBLISHED WITH A GIFT IN MEMORY OF

James Merrill

AND SUPPORT FROM ITS FOUNDING PATRONS

Sidney J. Weinberg, Jr. Foundation

The Berkley Foundation

Richard B. Fisher and Jeanne Donovan Fisher

Poems from the Women's Movement

EDITED BY
HONOR MOORE

AMERICAN POETS PROJECT

THE LIBRARY OF AMERICA

Some of the material in this volume is reprinted with permission of the holders of copyright and publication rights. Acknowledgments are on page 225.

The paper used in this publication meets the minimum requirements of the American National Standard for Information Sciences—Permanence of Paper for Printed Library Materials, ANSI Z39.48—1984.

Design by Chip Kidd and Mark Melnick.
Photo facing Contents: Honor Moore, 1973, © Jonathan Coppelman

Library of Congress Control Number: 2008943071
ISBN 978-1-59853-042-1
American Poets Project—28

First Printing

Poems from the Women's Movement

CONTENTS

INTRODUCTION

On a recent night I had supper with a friend, born like me in the era of World War II, a television executive and a woman whose life, like mine, was altered by feminism. "Tell me," I asked, "what you remember about poetry and the women's movement." I saw memory cross her face, and then she said a remarkable sentence: "The women's movement *was* poetry."

This is a collection that seeks to mark how women poets made a poetry that, in two decades, altered the face of American poetry forever. The volume includes 58 poets and nearly a hundred poems selected by one of those poets from a literature that is far more vast. "Let this coffin of verses inherit my pain," Joan Larkin wrote in "Rhyme of My Inheritance." Selecting poems written between the publication of Sylvia Plath's *Ariel* in the U.S. (1966) and 1982, I offer a portrait of how the inner lives of women came into language during that crucial decade and a half, as manifested in poems that range from furious to contemplative, outright funny to analytical, grief-stricken to visionary. A new language began—not a language that was linguistically new (although there are scholars who make that argument), but a language new to them. New to us, I should say, because in the process of speaking what was hidden, we began to identify with one another as women, to become a "we."

In 1966, when *Ariel* was published in the U.S., American women noticed. Not only women who ordinarily read poems, but housewives and mothers whose ambitions had awakened when they read Betty Friedan's *The Feminine Mystique* a few years earlier, and activists who came together to form the National Organization for Women (NOW) that same year. At the time, Plath was identified with the poets M. L. Rosenthal dubbed "confessional" in a 1959 review of Robert Lowell's *Life Studies*, but that label obscured the significance of her posthumous volume. Here was one woman, superbly trained in her craft, whose final poems uncompromisingly charted her rage, ambivalence, and grief in a voice with which many women identified.

While *Ariel* marked the beginning of a moment, there had been precursors. Between the wars, a feminist vision in poetry had flourished in the work of Gertrude Stein, H.D., and others, but by the 1960s, works like Stein's "Patriarchal Poetry" and H.D.'s *Helen in Egypt* did not appear in mainstream anthologies. There were also poems by women written during that period that denied the power of women. "Women have no wilderness in them," Louise Bogan wrote in a famous poem called "Women" (1923). That line, later derided by feminists, was followed by a catalogue of female inadequacy and lack of courage: "They wait, when they should turn to journeys." It would take women poets born in the decade in which Bogan wrote that poem to refute her. In 1963, Adrienne Rich completed "Snapshots of a Daughter-in-Law," a poem in which the speaker, a woman "content to glitter in fragments and rough drafts," moves from a "nervy" and "glowering" resentment, to emerge into her power, "her fine blades making the air wince."

Aesthetically, what women poets did in the 1970s could not have happened without the fissure in poetics that Modernism had effected in the previous decades. If one draws an analogy between the Victorian poetic excesses of formalism and ornate diction and the domestication that limited middle-class women in the 1950s, their enraged feminism and that of their daughters can be seen as a disruption analogous to Modernism and what came after. The Beats, beginning with Ginsberg's "Howl," exploded the boundaries even of free verse, allowing a full-bodied roar of emotion and protest; Black Mountain poets like Robert Creeley and Denise Levertov brought an intimacy of address to their poetry that enlarged the American vernacular that William Carlos Williams had introduced; and black poets like LeRoi Jones (Amiri Baraka) and Gwendolyn Brooks (leaving behind the idiom that in 1950 won her the first Pulitzer Prize ever given to an African-American) made poetry a vehicle for political rage.

As American women of the postwar generation came of age, they began to understand the repression their mothers had suffered, and as they imagined lives beyond the family, ownership of their own subjectivity followed. Just as the forms of women's protests ranged in style—from the Yippie-inspired Miss America pageant protest in September 1968 to the 1970 Fifth Avenue march marking the August 26 anniversary of woman suffrage—so, from the first moment, the new poems by women varied in strategy, appropriating a range of poetic approaches. From Marge Piercy's and Robin Morgan's satiric free verse, to Marilyn Hacker's subversive formalism, to Alice Notley's post-Modernism and Lucille Clifton's blues-inspired voicing of an African-American everywoman, women poets began to take up their experience directly, to gather for readings and in anthologies unified not by form or style, but by a common need to understand and change not only how women wrote poems, but how they used poems, and how they lived.

I moved to New York City in September 1969 and went to my first demonstration there that fall. It was on the bus to that march that I first heard of Robin Morgan, who as a child played Dagmar on *I Remember Mama*, a television show I had watched as a child, and who was now, I was amazed to hear, a poet and theorist of women's liberation. I had abandoned my college sonnets and was writing poems out of my own anger and 23-year-old unhappiness. The rich blood-hue of the female sign encircling a fist on the women's liberation button I bought on that bus ride, along with the certainty of the rhetoric in the women's journals I was reading, challenged the passivity of my poems, which lacked the audacity and certitude I admired in Sylvia Plath. As a student at Radcliffe, I had read Robert Lowell, but in reading Plath I encountered, as Alfred Stieglitz remarked on discovering Georgia O'Keeffe, a *woman* on paper. I did not imagine that my experience, a broken love affair with an older man and a secret abortion, could have the legitimacy of Plath's suicide. The women's movement would soon teach me otherwise.

At first it seemed that New York City in 1970 had no room for personal poems by privileged white women like me. The women's movement I tracked down was heavily influenced by the left politics I was familiar with, protesting racism, the war in Vietnam, inequity of rich and poor, all of which, women's liberation now declared, were consequences of male supremacy and patriarchy. Fulfilling the pledge I'd made when I quit graduate school, I took to the streets, and one day, hearing that the radical newspaper *Rat* had been taken over by a cadre of women guided by

WITCH (the Women's International Terrorist Conspiracy from Hell), of which Robin Morgan was a founder, I visited its offices on East 14th Street. There I found a book by the black poet Sonia Sanchez, whose fierce lyrics startled me with their directness and intimacy. It was there too, in the first woman-produced issue of *Rat*, that I read "Goodbye to All That," Robin Morgan's declaration of independence from the male left, its title borrowed from Robert Graves' 1929 anti-war memoir. Defending in polemic the takeover of a paper whose radicalism was compromised, she declared, by the pornography that drenched its pages, Morgan took on the sexism of the radical men for whom she and so many movement women had fetched coffee and typed flyers. "Sexism is not the fault of women—kill your fathers, not your mothers," she wrote. Goodbye to all that indeed.

Within a year, I'd found women who were constructing an activism that was woman-centered and independent of the left—the feminists, they were called. One group, Redstockings, held speak-outs about abortion and rape that were reported in the *Village Voice*, which also described the small groups women were forming in order to speak openly about their lives as women. I knew that I was not the only young woman who had kept an abortion secret, but in the small apartments where my own consciousness-raising group met, I heard other women's stories—not only of abortion, but of rape, motherhood, aspiration for other women, and for lives beyond the careers of their husbands and boyfriends. The aim of these groups was not merely to share intimate stories, but to find commonality and to analyze it, in order to understand how a woman's problem might not be hers alone, but part of her oppression under patriarchy. A new slogan was in the air—"the personal is political"—and in those rooms it seemed completely true.

We were meant to "speak bitter" as Chinese revolutionaries were said to have done, to discover who we were and what must be changed. "Eat rice have faith in women,/" the poet Fran Winant wrote, "what I don't know now/I still can learn." For some women, these groups guided how they moved in their work lives. In the group I entered in the spring of 1970, there were mothers starting day-care centers, women in the health professions, and women who were community organizers for whom perceptions from consciousness raising gave shape to new political and philosophical ideas. For those of us who were writers, aspects of our lives hidden from us were illuminated, becoming material for our writing. For all of us, what we had kept to ourselves because of competition with other women became instead a way to connect with one another.

We began to read differently as well. In this new context, Sylvia Plath was no longer an isolated victim, but the avatar of a new female literary consciousness. Among us, there were women already writing new poems we considered "in a woman's voice." I read poems by Audre Lorde that integrated her New York experience as an African-American woman into a politically engaged, insistent poetry rich with imagery and erotic force. And I read Diane Wakoski, whose poems transformed female resentment into long, finely articulated lyrics that turned on image and longing: "A woodpecker with fresh bloody crest/knocks/at my mouth. Father, for the first/time I say/your name. . . ." Now, too, there were women's literary magazines that published poems by women of my generation. I knew of *Aphra* in New York City, and in a women's bookstore I'd found the *Shameless Hussy Review* published in California and devoured the wry lyrics of Alta, its editor, and the poems of Susan Griffin, who in 1978 would publish her first book of feminist philosophy, *Woman and Nature: The Roaring Inside*

Her. In 1972, *Ms.*, the first glossy magazine with a feminist outlook, was founded, and in its pages, as in *Rat* and dozens of underground women's newspapers, there were always poems. Increasingly in my own work, I spoke not only with the directness and absence of shame gained in my CR group, but with humor and optimism inspired by the wave of women's politics and culture happening all around me. I began to write for other women, to seek poems in the life I was beginning to live, conscious of the ideas of feminism, trying, as Sharon Olds writes in her poem "Satan Says," "to write my/way out of the closed box."

I wrote without the company of other women poets until December 11, 1971, when I volunteered to take part in a women's poetry reading I'd seen advertised. The ground-floor room at the Loeb Student Center at NYU was packed, many of us sitting on the floor. Twenty-one women read—most of us had not published books and some, like me, had not published at all; others had appeared in *Rat*, *Moving Out*, and other women's liberation papers and journals; still others read work that had been, as I wrote later, "buried, as ladies' poems have been/in bureau drawers for years." The ecstatic, celebratory night ended only when the building closed. Six more group readings followed the next winter, and the year after we were joined by women poets like June Jordan, Sonia Sanchez, and Carolyn Kizer, whose books had been published by trade publishers. Kathryn Ruby and Lucille Iverson, who organized those readings, conceived an anthology they hoped would be definitive; but it was soon clear, as Iverson wrote, that their volume (published in 1974 as *We Become New*) could only be "a beginning representation of the heretofore muted voices of women."

*

Let us take those first NYU readings—and readings like them that were certainly happening elsewhere in the country—as the moment when women began to be aware that a strong wind was blowing through the hearts and minds of women writing poems, the moment we learned none of us was alone. It was at such readings, in crowded rooms all over New York City, among women who might otherwise not have read poems at all, that my friend, the television executive, encountered the women's movement she remembered 35 years later. In his preface to *Lyrical Ballads* (1800), Wordsworth, also inspired by a revolutionary moment, declared his intention "to choose incidents and situations from common life, and to relate or describe them, throughout, as far as was possible in a selection of language really used . . . and, at the same time, to throw over them a certain coloring of imagination." At those group readings, women read poems that sought to give value to their real lives, transforming them with the colors of an imagination that was woman-centered. One heard poems about fathers and mothers and sisters, about rape and women artists and Gertrude Stein, about miscarriages and the lost power of spinster aunts, about Milton's daughters and washing dishes, about the forbidden love of one woman for another, about Harriet Tubman and the subversive talk of waitresses, the love of mothers for sons and the yearning of daughters for common cause with their mothers. "But examine/this grief your mother/parades over our heads," Louise Glück wrote in a poem about Persephone and Demeter, "remembering/that she is one to whom/these depths were not offered."

Not only were women writing poems, they were making films and painting paintings and thinking about feminist approaches to architecture. In 1975, Knopf published *The New Woman's Survival Sourcebook*, edited by Kirsten

Ramstad and Susan Ronnie, that presented, in Whole-Earth-Catalog-like form, the panoply of women's culture, its profusion of magazines, newspapers, theaters, presses, food co-ops, credit unions, battered-women shelters, day-care centers—projects of women from every region in the United States, of women of color, and of lesbian women. The poetry section was introduced by my "Polemic #1"—"This is the poem to say 'Write poems, women' because I want to/read them"—and offered a double interview in which Robin Morgan and Adrienne Rich suggested that poetry, in Rich's words, "as much as journals and letters and diaries, has been an almost natural women's form. . . ." Rich also made the point that it was no accident that women novelists flourished in the 19th century—they disguised their real selves in fictional narratives—but now, because women could write openly as themselves, a new women's poetry was possible. Noting the group readings, Morgan credited the explosion of women's poetry to the new feminist tribe, linking it to the bardic tradition. What was new, Rich added, was that women were now publicly sharing their work, something that many of the past could not. "The poetry of many of my male contemporaries," she continued, "expresses the sense that we're all doomed to fail somehow. It's much more interesting to me to explore the condition of connectedness as a woman. Which is something absolutely new, unique historically, and finally so life enhancing. . . ."

At that moment, Rich was exploring that connectedness in a poem about a Soviet women's mountaineering team, all of whom had died on a climbing expedition in 1974. "Phantasia for Elvira Shatayev" might merely have been an elegy for the climbers, but instead the poet transforms them into an image of women undertaking something together—"a cable of blue fire ropes our bodies/burning together in the snow." While the work for change involved risk, separateness was a condition of danger from which women must now emerge. Unlike the women imagined in certain poems of the 1960s—like Anne Sexton's "The Ballad of the Lonely Masturbator" ("At night alone, I marry the bed") or Maxine Kumin's "At the End of the Affair" ("That it should end at an Albert Pick hotel/with the air conditioner gasping like a carp")— women were now reaching out to other women: "*till now*," Rich imagines Shatayev writing in a diary, "*we had not touched our strength* . . ."

Muriel Rukeyser, a generation older than Rich, had another response to the consequences of female isolation: "I'd rather be Muriel/than be dead and be Ariel." The two-line poem's title—"Not To Be Printed, Not To Be Said, Not To Be Thought"—acknowledged that to suggest that Plath had an option other than suicide or suffering was still taboo. But Rukeyser had her finger on a pulse—once women began to write poems, secure in the women's movement, they began to build a new tradition. Part of that task was seeking out examples of strength in women of the past—a column in *Ms.* called such women "foremothers." In a meditation on the life of the German political activist artist Käthe Kollwitz (1867–1945), Rukeyser asked, "What would happen if one woman told the truth about her life?" The answer she gave—"the world would split open"— resonates throughout this book, and throughout the history of women writers.

But it would take a few years for women to reread and find commonality in their poet foremothers. Many of us hadn't read women poets of the past. In the wake of Modernism and the New Criticism, professors required Eliot and Stevens and Pound; even women poets like Amy Lowell or Edna St. Vincent Millay, who'd had large readerships during their lifetimes, were absent from most college reading lists. When I took American poetry at Harvard in 1966, there were two women on the syllabus: Anne Bradstreet and Emily Dickinson. Even then I had the sense that if Bradstreet hadn't been the first significant American poet, she would not have been included; as for Dickinson, she was presented as a lone spinster with an accidental gift, and even as feminism turned me toward women of the past, I continued to buy into the interpretations I'd been taught. In that limited view, Elinor Wylie and Sara Teasdale seemed shrouded in Victorian lace, and I didn't bother to reread them. Lines like this by Wylie—"in coldest crucibles of pain/Her shrinking flesh was fired"—might once have salved heartbreak, but not now. Sara Teasdale "asked the heaven of stars/What I should give my love?" I preferred the heavens animated by Rich in her 1968 poem "Planetarium": "A woman in the shape of a monster/A monster in the shape of a woman/The skies are full of them." Claim monstrousness, claim our own difficult power, the poet seemed to be saying. Let yourself become "an instrument in the shape/of a woman trying to translate pulsations/into images for the relief of the body/and the reconstruction of the mind."

With the work of feminist critics, I would soon understand that many women poets had not only been left out of the canon, but also that selections in anthologies could distort the quality and nature of their achievement. I'd read feminist anthologies of 20th-century women's poetry like *No More Masks* and *Rising Tides*, but it was Louise Bernikow's comprehensive 1974 collection *The World Split Open: Four Centuries of Women Poets in England and America, 1550–1950* that, by retrieving poems from the past that asserted female power and value, rereading poets like Wylie and Amy Lowell, rediscovering poets like Frances E. W.

Harper and Adelaide Crapsey, and including blues singers like Ma Rainey and worker poets like Aunt Molly Jackson, introduced me to a possible canon of women poets. "What is commonly called literary history," Bernikow declared, "is actually a record of choices." And of interpretation: the following year, at the Donnell Library in New York, I heard Adrienne Rich give the lecture "Vesuvius at Home: The Power of Emily Dickinson" in which she presented the poet not as relegated to compensatory solitude but as a woman who made a choice to do her work, in the full knowledge that she was "a poet of genius."

"The woman's place of power within each of us is neither white nor surface; it is dark, it is ancient, and it is deep," Audre Lorde wrote in her essay "Poems Are Not Luxuries" (1977). "I speak here of poetry as a revelatory distillation of experience, not the sterile word play that, too often, the white fathers distorted the word poetry to mean —in order to cover a desperate wish for imagination without insight." Lorde's declaration reflected the increasing centrality of poetry to the women's movement. Reviewing a passel of women's poetry anthologies for *Ms.* in 1975, I'd read *Amazon Poetry*, an anthology edited by Joan Larkin and Elly Bulkin, which included a few of the poems in this book, among them Jan Clausen's "After Touch," which dramatizes her coming out with a startlingly positioned final line "I am a lesbian," and Martha Courtot's "I am a woman in ice/melting" that concludes with the lines "but now my fingers move/in a panic/of wanting to be burnt." The editors had sought to learn what lesbian poetry was, beyond love lyrics from one woman to another—the poems, they wrote, "belie a simple sexual definition." The collection included excerpts from an epic poem called "A Woman Is Talking to Death," first published in California in 1973.

I had picked up the green chapbook when the poet,

Judy Grahn, read the poem in its entirety at Westbeth, the artists' housing complex in Greenwich Village, late that year. With her woman lover on the Bay Bridge, the speaker of the poem comes upon the site of an accident—a white man on a motorcycle and a black man in a car have collided and the white man has died. The "queer" woman speaker of the poem leaves the black man behind despite his entreaties that she remain as his witness: "I left him as I have left so many of my lovers." As an unemployed lesbian, she has her own fears—the condition of the "unemployed lesbian" becomes a metaphor for the vulnerability of any woman unprotected by patriarchy in the face of its brute power—the bridge, the police, the motorcycle, the urban night. In the context, the speaker's admonition, "This woman is a lesbian, Be Careful" has a sharp irony, as does the "mock interrogation" the poet stages: "Have you ever held hands with a woman?" "Yes, many times." "Have you ever committed any indecent acts with women?" "Yes, many. I am guilty of allowing suicidal women to die before my eyes . . ." Over the course of eight sections, the poem opens into an examination of the boundary for women between love and the threat of violence, which the speaker personifies as Death: "wherever our own meat hangs on our own bones/for our own use/your pot is so empty/death, ho death/you shall be poor."

With this poem, the whole political enterprise of feminism was subsumed by poetic means into an understanding of the complexity of the stark power relations that involve gender, race, and sexuality. In the hush that fell on the room at Westbeth after Grahn finished reading, I felt the poem both as a caution that we not allow our poems to become merely parochial and a demonstration of the poetic force we now had at our disposal. It is in light of the challenge of "A Woman Is Talking to Death" that I now read Lorde's "To a Woman in Rage" in which the black speaker, a lesbian who has a white lover, hallucinates her own racist murder of a white woman—"her white face dangles/a tapestry of disasters seen/ Through a veneer of order." Or June Jordan's "Case in Point," an account of a rape of a black woman by a black man. Or Diane Di Prima's "Annunciation," in which the originating moment of the birth of Christ is read as rape. When Audre Lorde wrote in her essay that for women "poetry is not a luxury," she was speaking for a movement that read its writers. "It is a vital necessity of our existence. It forms the quality of the light within which we predicate our hopes and dreams toward survival and change, first made into language, then into idea, then into more tangible action."

As the 1970s progressed, women poets began to have an impact in the mainstream of American literary life. In 1974, when Adrienne Rich was chosen co-winner with Allen Ginsberg of the National Book Award, she accepted the prize, by prior agreement, with two of the other women nominated, Alice Walker and Audre Lorde. In 1976, Stanley Kunitz chose Carolyn Forché as the winner of the prestigious Yale Younger Poets prize, and her volume opened with "Burning the Tomato Worms," a long poem in which a young woman claims strength from the ambiguous legacy of her immigrant grandmother; the following year, 1977, he chose Olga Broumas's *Beginning with O*, a young woman's reading of Greek myth that also celebrated the erotic love of women. A line declaring a woman's sexual desire for another woman might now no longer have the axis-shifting resonance it had just a few years before. The poems women were now writing might find themselves, as Jorie Graham writes, "opening/from eternity//to privacy . . ."

In the 1950s, the poet Jane Cooper, born a decade before Plath, had censored her second collection of poems, recovering it only when riffling through a box of old papers decades later. Unmarried and childless, she had nonetheless felt she could not be a poet. "Privately I felt the poems were never finished. I suspect most privately of all, that I couldn't face living out the range of intuition they revealed." Encouraged by women friends, including Adrienne Rich, Jean Valentine, and Muriel Rukeyser, she published those poems in 1974, with an essay explaining her anguished journey toward making them public. The issue was not so much the poems themselves, but the poet's reticence, her resistance to moving from being a girl who wrote to a woman poet. How could she live the life of a woman and the life of a poet? This is a question women poets still ask, but it is a measure of the distance we came in the years this book covers, that Cooper, by then the author of several volumes of poems, could write, in 1982, what amounts to a declaration of a poet's freedom:

. . . . . It seems I am on the edge
of discovering the green notebook containing the poems
    of my life,
I mean the ones I never wrote. The meadow turns
    intensely green.
The notebook is under my fingers. I read. My
    companions read.
Now thunder joins in, scurry of leaves. . . .

Honor Moore

SYLVIA PLATH | 1932–1963

The Applicant

First, are you our sort of a person?
Do you wear
A glass eye, false teeth or a crutch,
A brace or a hook,
Rubber breasts or a rubber crotch,

Stitches to show something's missing? No, no? Then
How can we give you a thing?
Stop crying.
Open your hand.
Empty? Empty. Here is a hand

To fill it and willing
To bring teacups and roll away headaches
And do whatever you tell it.
Will you marry it?
It is guaranteed

To thumb shut your eyes at the end
And dissolve of sorrow.
We make new stock from the salt.
I notice you are stark naked.
How about this suit——

Black and stiff, but not a bad fit.
Will you marry it?
It is waterproof, shatterproof, proof
Against fire and bombs through the roof.
Believe me, they'll bury you in it.

Now your head, excuse me, is empty.
I have the ticket for that.
Come here, sweetie, out of the closet.
Well, what do you think of *that*?
Naked as paper to start

But in twenty-five years she'll be silver,
In fifty, gold.
A living doll, everywhere you look.
It can sew, it can cook,
It can talk, talk, talk.

It works, there is nothing wrong with it.
You have a hole, it's a poultice.
You have an eye, it's an image.
My boy, it's your last resort.
Will you marry it, marry it, marry it.

11 October 1962

DIANE WAKOSKI | 1937–

The Father of My Country

All fathers in Western civilization must have
a military origin. The
ruler,
governor,
yes,
he is
was the
general at one time or other.
And George Washington
won the hearts
of his country—the rough military man
with awkward
sincere
drawing-room manners.

My father;
have you ever heard me speak of him? I seldom
do. But I had a father,
and he had military origins—or my origins from
him
are military,
militant. That is, I remember him only in uniform. But
    of the navy,

30 years a chief petty officer,
Always away from home.

It is rough/hard for me to
speak now.
I'm not used to talking
about him.
Not used to
naming his objects/
objects
that never surrounded me.

A woodpecker with fresh bloody crest
knocks
at my mouth. Father, for the first
time I say
your name. Name rolled in thick Polish parchment
    scrolls,
name of Roman candle drippings when I sit at my table
alone, each night,
name of naval uniforms and name of
telegrams, name of
coming home from your aircraft carrier,
name of shiny shoes,
name of Hawaiian dolls, name
of mess spoons, name of greasy machinery, and name of
stencilled names.
Is it your blood I carry in a test tube,
my arm,
to let fall, crack, and spill on the sidewalk
in front of the men

I know,
I love,
I know, and
want? So you left my house when I was under two,
being replaced by other machinery, and
I didn't believe you left me.

      This scene: the trunk yielding treasures of
      a green fountain pen, heart-shaped mirror,
      amber beads, old letters with brown ink, and
      the gopher snake stretched across the palm tree
      in the front yard with woody trunk like monkey
          skins,
      and a sunset through the skinny persimmon
          trees. You
      came walking, not even a telegram or post card
          from
      Tahiti. Love, love, through my heart like ink in
      the thickest nubbed pen, black and flowing into
          words.
      You came to me, and I at least six. Six doilies
      of lace, six battleship cannon, six old beerbottles,
      six thick steaks, six love letters, six clocks running
      backwards, six watermelons, and six baby teeth, a
          six
      cornered hat on six men's heads, six lovers at once
      or one lover at sixes and sevens; how I confuse
      all this with my
      dream
      walking the tightrope bridge
      with gold knots

over
the mouth of an anemone/ tissue spiral lips
and holding on so that the ropes burned
as if my wrists had been tied

If George Washington
had not
been the Father
of my Country,
it is doubtful that I would ever have
found
a father. Father in my mouth, on my lips, in my
tongue, out of all my womanly fire,
Father I have left in my steel filing cabinet as a name on
     my birth
certificate, Father, I have left in the teeth pulled out at
dentists' offices and thrown into their garbage cans,
Father living in my wide cheekbones and short feet,
Father in my Polish tantrums and my American speech,
     Father, not a
holy name, not a name I cherish but the name I bear, the
     name
that makes me one of a kind in any phone book because
you changed it, and nobody
but us
has it,
Father who makes me dream in the dead of night of the
     falling cherry
blossoms, Father who makes me know all men will leave me
if I love them,
Father who made me a maverick,

a writer
a namer,
name/father, sun/father, moon/father, bloody mars /
    father,

other children said, "My father is a doctor,"
or
"My father gave me this camera,"
or
"My father took me to
the movies,"
or
"My father and I went swimming,"
but
my father is coming in a letter
once a month
for a while,
and my father
sometimes came in a telegram
but
mostly
my father came to me
in sleep, my father because I dreamed in one night that I
    dug through
the ash heap in back of the pepper tree and found a
    diamond shaped like
a dog and my father called the dog and it came leaping
    over to him and
he walked away out of the yard down the road with the
    dog jumping
and yipping at his heels,

my father was not in the telephone book
in my city;
my father was not sleeping with my mother
at home;
my father did not care if I studied the
piano;
my father did not care what
I did;
and I thought my father was handsome and I loved him
and I wondered
why
he left me alone so much,
so many years
in fact, but
my father
made me what I am
a lonely woman
without a purpose, just as I was
a lonely child
without any father. I walked with words, words, and
names,
names. Father was not
one of my words.
Father was not
one of my names. But now I say, George you have
become my father,
in his 20th century naval uniform. George Washington,
I need your
love; George, I want to call you Father, Father, my
Father,
Father of my country,

that is

me. And I say the name to chant it. To sing it. To lace it
        around me

like weaving cloth. Like a happy child on that shining
        afternoon in

the palmtree sunset with her mother's trunk yielding
        treasures,

I cry and

cry,

Father,

Father,

Father,

have you really come home?

Käthe Kollwitz

1

Held between wars
my lifetime
           among wars, the big hands of the world of death
my lifetime
listens to yours.

The faces of the sufferers
in the street, in dailiness,
their lives showing
through their bodies
a look as of music
the revolutionary look
that says   I am in the world
to change the world
my lifetime
is to love to endure to suffer the music
to set its portrait
up as a sheet of the world
the most moving the most alive
Easter and bone
and Faust walking among flowers of the world
and the child alive within the living woman, music of man,

and death holding my lifetime between great hands
the hands of enduring life
that suffers the gifts and madness of full life, on earth, in
    our time,
and through my life, through my eyes, through my arms
    and hands
may give the face of this music in portrait waiting for
the unknown person
held in the two hands, you.

2

Woman as gates, saying:
"The process is after all like music,
like the development of a piece of music.
The fugues come back and
                          again and again
interweave.
A theme may seem to have been put aside,
but it keeps returning—
the same thing modulated,
somewhat changed in form.
Usually richer.
And it is very good that this is so."

A woman pouring her opposites.
"After all there are happy things in life too.
Why do you show only the dark side?"
"I could not answer this. But I know—
in the beginning my impulse to know
the working life
              had little to do with

pity or sympathy.
                    I simply felt
that the life of the workers was beautiful."

She said, "I am groping in the dark."

She said, "When the door opens, of sensuality,
then you will understand it too. The struggle begins.
Never again to be free of it,
often you will feel it to be your enemy.
Sometimes
you will almost suffocate,
such joy it brings."

Saying of her husband: "My wish
is to die after Karl.
I know no person who can love as he can,
with his whole soul.
But often too it has made me
so terribly happy."

She said: "We rowed over to Carrara at dawn,
climbed up to the marble quarries
and rowed back at night. The drops of water
fell like glittering stars
from our oars."

She said: "As a matter of fact,
I believe
            that bisexuality
is almost   a necessary factor

in artistic production; at any rate,
the tinge of masculinity within me
helped me
        in my work."

She said: "The only technique I can still manage.
It's hardly a technique at all, lithography.
In it
    only the essentials count."

A tight-lipped man in a restaurant last night saying to me:
"Kollwitz?   She's too black-and-white."

3

Held among wars, watching
    all of them
    all these people
    weavers,
    Carmagnole

Looking at
    all of them
    death, the children
    patients in waiting-rooms
    famine
    the street

A woman seeing
    the violent, inexorable
    movement of nakedness
    and the confession of No

the confession of great weakness, war,
all streaming to one son killed, Peter;
even the son left living; repeated,
the father, the mother; the grandson
another Peter killed in another war; firestorm;
dark, light, as two hands,
this pole and that pole as the gates.

What would happen if one woman told the truth about
    her life?
    The world would split open

4   Song : The Calling-Up

Rumor, stir of ripeness
rising within this girl
sensual blossoming
of meaning, its light and form.

The birth-cry summoning
out of the male, the father
from the warm woman
a mother in response.

The word of death
calls up the fight with stone
wrestle with grief with time
from the material make
an art harder than bronze.

Mouth looking directly at you
eyes in their inwardness looking
directly at you
half light   half darkness
woman, strong, German, young artist
flows into
wide sensual mouth meditating
looking right at you
eyes shadowed with brave hand
looking deep at you
flows into
wounded brave mouth
grieving and hooded eyes
alive, German, in her first War
flows into
strength of the worn face
a skein of lines
broods, flows into
mothers among the war graves
bent over death
facing the father
stubborn upon the field
flows into
the marks of her knowing—
Nie Wieder Krieg
repeated in the eyes
flows into
"Seedcorn must not be ground"
and the grooved cheek
lips drawn fine

the down-drawn grief
face of our age
flows into
Pieta, mother and
between her knees
life as her son in death
pouring from the sky of
one more war
flows into
face almost obliterated
hand over the mouth forever
hand over one eye now
the other great eye
closed

Not To Be Printed, Not To Be Said, Not To Be Thought

I'd rather be Muriel
than be dead and be Ariel.

ADRIENNE RICH | 1929–

Planetarium

Thinking of Caroline Herschel (1750–1848)
astronomer, sister of William; and others.

A woman in the shape of a monster
a monster in the shape of a woman
the skies are full of them

a woman   'in the snow
among the Clocks and instruments
or measuring the ground with poles'

in her 98 years to discover
8 comets

she whom the moon ruled
like us
levitating into the night sky
riding the polished lenses

Galaxies of women, there
doing penance for impetuousness
ribs chilled
in those spaces   of the mind

An eye,

'virile, precise and absolutely certain'
from the mad webs of Uranusborg

                    encountering the NOVA

every impulse of light exploding
from the core
as life flies out of us

        Tycho whispering at last
        'Let me not seem to have lived in vain'

What we see, we see
and seeing is changing

the light that shrivels a mountain
and leaves a man alive

Heartbeat of the pulsar
heart sweating through my body

The radio impulse
pouring in from Taurus

        I am bombarded yet   I stand

I have been standing all my life in the
direct path of a battery of signals
the most accurately transmitted most
untranslatable language in the universe
I am a galactic cloud so deep   so invo-

luted that a light wave could take 15
years to travel through me   And has
taken   I am an instrument in the shape
of a woman trying to translate pulsations
into images   for the relief of the body
and the reconstruction of the mind.

Diving into the Wreck

First having read the book of myths,
and loaded the camera,
and checked the edge of the knife-blade,
I put on
the body-armor of black rubber
the absurd flippers
the grave and awkward mask.
I am having to do this
not like Cousteau with his
assiduous team
aboard the sun-flooded schooner
but here alone.

There is a ladder.
The ladder is always there
hanging innocently
close to the side of the schooner.
We know what it is for,
we who have used it.
Otherwise

it's a piece of maritime floss
some sundry equipment.

I go down.
Rung after rung and still
the oxygen immerses me
the blue light
the clear atoms
of our human air,
I go down.
My flippers cripple me,
I crawl like an insect down the ladder
and there is no one
to tell me when the ocean
will begin.

First the air is blue and then
it is bluer and then green and then
black I am blacking out and yet
my mask is powerful
it pumps my blood with power
the sea is another story
the sea is not a question of power
I have to learn alone
to turn my body without force
in the deep element.

And now: it is easy to forget
what I came for
among so many who have always
lived here
swaying their crenellated fans

between the reefs
and besides
you breathe differently down here.

I came to explore the wreck.
The words are purposes.
The words are maps.
I came to see the damage that was done
and the treasures that prevail.
I stroke the beam of my lamp
slowly along the flank
of something more permanent
than fish or weed

the thing I came for:
the wreck and not the story of the wreck
the thing itself and not the myth
the drowned face always staring
toward the sun
the evidence of damage
worn by salt and sway into this threadbare beauty
the ribs of the disaster
curving their assertion
among the tentative haunters.

This is the place.
And I am here, the mermaid whose dark hair
streams black, the merman in his armored body
We circle silently
about the wreck
we dive into the hold.
I am she: I am he

whose drowned face sleeps with open eyes
whose breasts still bear the stress
whose silver, copper, vermeil cargo lies
obscurely inside barrels
half-wedged and left to rot
we are the half-destroyed instruments
that once held to a course
the water-eaten log
the fouled compass

We are, I am, you are
by cowardice or courage
the one who find our way
back to this scene
carrying a knife, a camera
a book of myths
in which
our names do not appear.

Phantasia for Elvira Shatayev

Leader of a women's climbing team, all of whom died in a storm on Lenin Peak, August 1974. Later, Shatayev's husband found and buried the bodies.

The cold felt cold until our blood
grew colder   then the wind
died down and we slept
If in this sleep I speak
it's with a voice no longer personal
(I want to say   *with voices*)

When the wind tore   our breath from us at last
we had no need of words
For months   for years   each one of us
had felt her own *yes*   growing in her
slowly forming   as she stood at windows   waited
for trains   mended her rucksack   combed her hair
What we were to learn   was simply   what we had
up here   as out of all words   that *yes*   gathered
its forces   fused itself   and only just in time
to meet a *No* of no degrees
the black hole   sucking the world in

I feel you climbing toward me
your cleated bootsoles leaving   their geometric bite
colossally embossed   on microscopic crystals
as when I trailed you in the Caucasus
Now I am further
ahead   than either of us dreamed   anyone would be
I have become
the white snow packed like asphalt by the wind
the women I love   lightly flung   against the mountain
that blue sky
our frozen eyes unribboned   through the storm
we could have stitched that blueness   together   like a
    quilt

You come (I know this) with your love   your loss
strapped to your body   with your tape-recorder   camera
ice-pick   against advisement
to give us burial in the snow   and in your mind
While my body lies out here

flashing like a prism   into your eyes
how could you sleep   You climbed here for yourself
we climbed for ourselves

When you have buried us   told your story
ours does not end   we stream
into the unfinished   the unbegun
the possible
Every cell's core of heat   pulsed out of us
into the thin air   of the universe
the armature of rock beneath these snows
this mountain   which has taken   the imprint of our
        minds
through changes elemental and minute
as those we underwent
to bring each other here
choosing ourselves   each other   and this life
whose every breath   and grasp   and further foothold
is somewhere   still enacted   and continuing

In the diary I wrote: *Now we are ready*
and each of us knows it   I have never loved
like this   I have never seen
my own forces so taken up and shared
and given back
After the long training   the early sieges
we are moving almost effortlessly in our love

In the diary as the wind   began to tear
at the tents over us   I wrote:
We know now we have always been in danger

down in our separateness
and now up here together   but till now
we had not touched our strength

In the diary torn from my fingers I had written:
What does love mean
what does it mean   "to survive"
A cable of blue fire ropes our bodies
burning together in the snow   We will not live
to settle for less   We have dreamed of this
all of our lives

The Ballad of
the Lonely Masturbator

The end of the affair is always death.
She's my workshop. Slippery eye,
out of the tribe of myself my breath
finds you gone. I horrify
those who stand by. I am fed.
At night, alone, I marry the bed.

Finger to finger, now she's mine.
She's not too far. She's my encounter.
I beat her like a bell. I recline
in the bower where you used to mount her.
You borrowed me on the flowered spread.
At night, alone, I marry the bed.

Take for instance this night, my love,
that every single couple puts together
with a joint overturning, beneath, above,
the abundant two on sponge and feather,
kneeling and pushing, head to head.
At night alone, I marry the bed.

I break out of my body this way,
an annoying miracle. Could I
put the dream market on display?
I am spread out. I crucify.
My little plum is what you said.
At night, alone, I marry the bed.

Then my black-eyed rival came.
The lady of water, rising on the beach,
a piano at her fingertips, shame
on her lips and a flute's speech.
And I was the knock-kneed broom instead.
At night, alone, I marry the bed.

ALICIA OSTRIKER | 1937–

The Anniversary

Of course we failed, by succeeding.
The fiery cherub becomes his smothering.
A greedy heart dives into a dream
Of power or truth, and wakes up middle-aged
In some committee room.
It is eating paper instead of God.
We two are one, my bird, this is a wedding.

When love was war, you swore you'd burn
Your life and die at thirty-five. I said good riddance,
Bright hairy boy, I will beat you, down,
Tear you to monkey shreds, survive like earth,
Owl-eyed, because I wanted to see everything
Black and permanent and kill you with your theories.
We used to wake up sweaty and entangled.

Thirty, home, and work. We cohabit in a functioning
    machine.
There is violence, somewhere else. Do we wish this? It
    occurs,
The flayed combatant, the dismembered child,
The instruments in the basement. We must wish it. See,
Between us is peace, our babies are plump,
I know you, I caress you, I fail you. My faith adheres
In nothing. Don't leave me, don't leave me.

SONIA SANCHEZ | 1934–

personal letter #2

I speak skimpily to
you about apartments I
no longer dwell in
and children who
chant their dis
obedience in choruses.
If I were young
I wd stretch you
with my wild words
while our nights
run soft with hands.
But I am what I
am, woman, alone
amid all this noise

a poem for my father

how sad it must be
to love so many women
to need so many black
perfumed bodies weeping
underneath you.
                    when i remember all those nights
i filled my mind with
long wars between short
sighted trojans & greeks
while you slapped some
wide hips about in
your pvt dungeon,
when i remember your
deformity   i want to
do something about your
makeshift manhood.
i guess
        that is why
on meeting your sixth
wife, i cross myself
with her confessionals.

MISCARRIAGE

let's try again
lots more where that came from
ha ha
don't say "lost" the baby,
sounds like you misplaced it.
"let's see, i had it here
a couple of days ago. . . ."

10 commandments for liberation

1 • thou shalt clean up thine own messes.
no servants whether paid (cleaning ladies)
or indentured (wives).

2 • thou shalt not use other people. as tom
hayden used james rector to advertise
people's park, as marxists use workers
to overthro the ruling class, as i just
used tom hayden for demonstration purposes.

3 • thou shalt not foul. the air, with motor
vehicles, the water, with detergents,
the earth, with chemicals and pesticides.

4 • thou shalt not deny any person's
humanity. blacks are not niggers, vietnamese
are not gooks, women are not chicks,
cops are not pigs.

5 • thou shalt not endanger other people
for an idea.

6 • thou shalt not be ashamed, we are all
perverts. we all have pasts we could spend
our whole lives denying.

7 • thou shalt revel in what you really are:
don't change your looks, don't stop
talking, go ahead and be.

8 • listen to your body: it will let you
know whether or not you are content

9 • living things shall be allowed to
breathe & grow.

10 • write your own commandments. i am only
a person like you. "burn this
& memorize yourself."

Euridice

all the male poets write of orpheus
as if they look back & expect
to find me walking patiently
behind them. they claim i fell into hell.
damn them, i say.
i stand in my own pain
& sing my own song.

miss rosie

When I watch you
wrapped up like garbage
sitting, surrounded by the smell
of too old potato peels
or
when I watch you
in your old man's shoes
with the little toe cut out
sitting, waiting for your mind
like next week's grocery
I say
when I watch you
you wet brown bag of a woman
who used to be the best looking gal in Georgia
used to be called the Georgia Rose
I stand up
through your destruction
I stand up

the lost baby poem

the time i dropped your almost body down
down to meet the waters under the city
and run one with the sewage to the sea
what did i know about waters rushing back
what did i know about drowning
or being drowned

you would have been born into winter
in the year of the disconnected gas
and no car   we would have made the thin
walk over Genesee hill into the Canada wind
to watch you slip like ice into strangers' hands
you would have fallen naked as snow into winter
if you were here i could tell you these
and some other things

if i am ever less than a mountain
for your definite brothers and sisters
let the rivers pour over my head
let the sea take me for a spiller
of seas   let black men call me stranger
always   for your never named sake

MAXINE KUMIN | 1925–

At the End of the Affair

That it should end in an Albert Pick hotel
with the air conditioner gasping like a carp
and the bathroom tap plucking its one-string harp
and the sourmash bond half gone in the open bottle,

that it should end in this stubborn disarray
of stockings and car keys and suitcases,
all the unfoldings that came forth yesterday
now crammed back to overflow their spaces,

considering the hairsbreadth accident of touch
the nightcap leads to—how it protracts
the burst of colors, the sweetgrass of two tongues,
then turns the lock in Hilton or in Sheraton,
in Marriott or Holiday Inn for such
a man and woman—bearing in mind these facts,

better to break glass, sop with towels, tear
snapshots up, pour whiskey down the drain
than reach and tangle in the same old snare
saying the little lies again.

MAY SWENSON | 1913–1989

O'Keeffe Retrospective

Into the sacral cavity can fit the skull of a deer,
the vertical pleat in the snout, place of the yoni.
Within the embrasure of antlers that flare, sensitive
tips like fingers defining thighs and hips, inner horns
hold ovary curls of space.

Where a white bead rolls at the fulcrum of widening
    knees,
black dawn evolves, a circular saw of polished speed;
its bud, like Mercury, mad in its whiz, shines, although
stone jaws of the same delta, opposite, lock agape—
blunt monolithic hinge, stranded, grand, tide gone out.

A common boundary has hip and hill, sky and pelvic basin.
From the upright cleft, shadow-entwirled, early veils
of spectral color—a tender maypole, girlish, shy, unbraids
to rainbow streams slowly separated.

A narrow eye on end, the lily's riper crack of bloom:
stamen stiff, it lengthens, swells, at its ball (walled pupil)
a sticky tear of sap. Shuttlecock (divided muzzle of the
    dried

deer's face, eyeholes outline the ischium) is, in the flap of
the jack-in-the-pulpit, silken flesh. As windfolds of
the mesa (regal, opulent odalisque) are, saturate orange,
    sunset.

Cerulean is solid. Clouds are tiles, or floats of ice
a cobalt spa melts. Evaporating, they yet grip their shapes;
if walked on, prove not fluff and steam. These clouds
are hard. Then rock may be pillow, stones vacant spaces.
Look into the hole: it will bulk. Hold the rock: it will
    empty.

Opposite, the thousand labia of a gray rose puff apart,
like smoke, yet they have a fixed, or nearly fixed, union,
skeletal, innominate, but potent to implode, flush red,
tighten to a first bud-knot, single, sacral.
Not quite closed, the cruciform fissure in the deer's
nose bone, symphysis of the pubis.

Where inbetweens turn visible blues, white objects
    vanish,
except—see, high at horizon on a vast canvas sky—
one undisciplined tuft, little live cloud, blowing:
fleece, breath of illusion.

ERICA JONG | 1942–

Why I Died

She is the woman I follow.
Whenever I enter a room
she has been there—

> with her hair smelling of lions & tigers,
> with her dress blacker than octopus ink,
> with her shoes moving like lizards
> over the waving wheat of the rug.

Sometimes I think of her as my mother
but she died by her own hand
before I was born.

> She drowned in the waves of her own hair.
> She strangled on Isadora's scarf.
> She suckled a poisonous snake at her breast
> like Cleopatra or Eve.

She is no virgin & no madonna.
Her eyelids are purple.
She sleeps around.

Wherever I go I meet her lovers.
Wherever I go I hear their stories.
Wherever I go they tell me
different versions of her suicide.

I sleep with them in gratitude.
I sleep with them to make them tell.
I sleep with them as punishment or reward.

She is the woman I follow.
I wear her cast-off clothes.
She is my mother, my daughter.
She is writing this suicide note.

RITA MAE BROWN | 1944–

Sappho's Reply

My voice rings down through thousands of years
To coil around your body and give you strength,
You who have wept in direct sunlight,
Who have hungered in invisible chains,
Tremble to the cadence of my legacy:
An army of lovers shall not fail.

SUSAN GRIFFIN | 1943–

I Like to Think of Harriet Tubman

I like to think of Harriet Tubman.
Harriet Tubman who carried a revolver,
who had a scar on her head from a rock thrown
by a slave-master (because she
talked back), and who
had a ransom on her head
of thousands of dollars and who
was never caught, and who
had no use for the law
when the law was wrong,
who defied the law. I like
to think of her.
I like to think of her especially
when I think of the problem of
feeding children.

The legal answer
to the problem of feeding children
is ten free lunches every month,
being equal, in the child's real life,
to eating lunch every other day.
Monday but not Tuesday.
I like to think of the President
eating lunch Monday, but not

Tuesday.
And when I think of the President
and the law, and the problem of
feeding children, I like to
think of Harriet Tubman
and her revolver.

And then sometimes
I think of the President
and other men,
men who practice the law,
who revere the law,
who make the law,
who enforce the law,
who live behind
and operate through
and feed themselves
at the expense of
starving children
because of the law.

Men who sit in paneled offices
and think about vacations
and tell women
whose care it is
to feed children
not to be hysterical
not to be hysterical as in the word
hysterikos, the greek for
womb suffering,
not to suffer in their

wombs,
not to care,
not to bother the men
because they want to think
of other things
and do not want
to take the women seriously.
I want them
to take women seriously.
I want them to think about Harriet Tubman,
and remember,
remember she was beat by a white man
and she lived
and she lived to redress her grievances,
and she lived in swamps
and wore the clothes of a man
bringing hundreds of fugitives from
slavery, and was never caught,
and led an army,
and won a battle,
and defied the laws
because the laws were wrong, I want men
to take us seriously.
I am tired wanting them to think
about right and wrong.
I want them to fear.
I want them to feel fear now
as I have felt suffering in the womb, and
I want them
to know
that there is always a time

there is always a time to make right
what is wrong,
there is always a time
for retribution
and that time
is beginning.

Three Poems for Women

1

This is a poem for a woman doing dishes.
This is a poem for a woman doing dishes.
It must be repeated.
It must be repeated,
again and again,
again and again,
because the woman doing dishes
because the woman doing dishes
has trouble hearing
has trouble hearing.

2

And this is another poem for a woman
cleaning the floor
who cannot hear at all.
Let us have a moment of silence
for the woman who cleans the floor.

And here is one more poem
for the woman at home
with children.
You never see her at night.
Stare at an empty space and imagine her there,
the woman with children
because she cannot be here to speak
for herself,
and listen
to what you think
she might say.

An Answer to a Man's Question, "What Can I Do About Women's Liberation?"

Wear a dress.
Wear a dress that you made yourself, or bought in a
    dress store.
Wear a dress and underneath the dress wear elastic,
    around
your hips, and underneath your nipples.
Wear a dress and underneath the dress wear a sanitary
    napkin.
Wear a dress and wear sling-back, high-heeled shoes.
Wear a dress, with elastic and a sanitary napkin
    underneath,
and sling-back shoes on your feet, and walk down
    Telegraph Avenue.

4

Wear a dress, with elastic and a sanitary napkin and sling-
back shoes on Telegraph Avenue and try to run.

Find a man.
Find a nice man who you would like to ask you for a date.
Find a nice man who *will* ask you for a date.
Keep your dress on.
Ask the nice man who asks you for a date to come to
    dinner.
Cook the nice man a nice dinner so the dinner is ready
    before
he comes and your dress is nice and clean and wear a
    smile.
Tell the nice man you're a virgin, or you don't have
birth control, or you would like to get to know him
    better.
Keep your dress on.
Go to the movies by yourself.

Find a job.
Iron your dress.
Wear your ironed dress and promise the boss you won't
    get
pregnant (which in your case is predictable) and you
    like to
type, and be sincere and wear your smile.
Find a job or get on welfare.
Borrow a child and get on welfare.
Borrow a child and stay in the house all day with the child,
or go to the public park with the child, and take the child

to the welfare office and cry and say your man left you and
be humble and wear your dress and your smile, and don't talk
back, keep your dress on, cook more nice dinners, stay
away from Telegraph Avenue, and still, you won't know the
half of it, not in a million years.

ROBIN MORGAN | 1941–

Quotations from Charwoman Me

You never asked to be a master
and God knows (if She would only say so)
that I never asked to be a slave.
Position papers, grocery lists
rain down like ticker-tape on my long-march procession
past where you cheer me on,
waving from the wistful side of—let's admit it—
barricades.

You're tired of living without any joy.
You think you're going crazy.
You need my friendship.
You're afraid to demand the right
to be afraid.
You're trying very hard.
I know that, and you can't imagine
how I wish it were enough.

I need to sleep.
I never asked for this;
you never asked.
Our twenty-five-inch son
whimpers in the night
and my breasts hurt until I wake myself
and feed him.

He never asked for anything at all.
We all want just to be a little happy.

Listen, I see an older me, alone
in some room, busy on the telephone
dialing all my terrible truths.
This thing has never let me live
as we both know I might have; yet I see
this thing can cut me down
on some street or podium tomorrow—
or just let me live, alone.

Our child looks back and forth
from your face into mine, and laughs.
You worry about us, wondering if
something within us has broken.
You hold my body as if it were glass
that will cut you.
I'd stop this if I could, believe me, my beloved.
I'm dying of bitterness.
I love your forehead.
Did I ever tell you that?

Matrilineal Descent

Not having spoken for years now,
I know you claim exile from my consciousness.
Yet I wear mourning whole nights through
for that embrace that warmed my ignorant lust

even past intimacies you had dreamed.
I played your daughter-husband, lover-son, to earn
both Abraham and Ishmael's guilt
for your indulgence, and in time, reproach.
Who sent us to that wilderness we both now know,
although I blamed you for that house of women
too many years. But Time is a waiting woman,
not some old man with a stupid beard,
and when I finally met my father I found him
arrogant and dull, a formican liar
with an Austrian accent. Well, we meet
the phantom that we long for in the end,
and getting there is half the grief.
Meanwhile, my theories rearrange themselves
like sand before this woman whose flaccid breasts
sway with her stumblings, whose diamonds
still thaw pity from my eyes.
You're older than I thought. But so am I,
and grateful that we've come to this:
a ragged truce, an affirmation in me
that your strength, your pushiness, your sharp love,
your embroidery of lies—all, all were survival tools,
as when, during our personal diaspora, you stood
in some far country blocks away,
burning poems I no longer sent you
like Yahrzeit candles in my name, unsure of me at last
who sought a birthright elsewhere,
beyond the oasis of your curse,
even beyond that last mirage, your blessing.
Mother, in ways neither of us can ever understand,
I have come home.

CYNTHIA MACDONALD | 1928–

Objets d'Art

When I was seventeen, a man in the Dakar Station
Men's Room (I couldn't read the signs) said to me:
You're a real ball cutter. I thought about that
For months and finally decided
He was right. Once I knew that was my thing,
Or whatever we would have said in those days,
I began to perfect my methods. Until then
I had never thought of trophies. Preservation
Was at first a problem: pickling worked
But was a lot of trouble. Freezing
Proved to be the answer. I had to buy
A second freezer just last year; the first
Was filled with rows and rows of
Pink and purple lumps encased in Saran wrap.

I have more subjects than I can handle,
But only volunteers. It is an art like hypnosis
Which cannot be imposed on the unwilling victim.
If you desire further information about the process and
The benefits, please drop in any night from nine to
        twelve.
My place is east of Third on Fifty-sixth.
You'll know it by the three gold ones over the door.

For My Sister Molly Who in the Fifties

Once made a fairy rooster from
Mashed potatoes
Whose eyes I forget
But green onions were his tail
And his two legs were carrot sticks
A tomato slice his crown.
Who came home on vacation
When the sun was hot
and cooked
and cleaned
And minded least of all
The children's questions
A million or more
Pouring in on her
Who had been to school
And knew (and told us too) that certain
Words were no longer good
And taught me not to say us for we
No matter what "Sonny said" up the
road.

FOR MY SISTER MOLLY WHO IN THE FIFTIES
Knew Hamlet well and read into the night
And coached me in my songs of Africa

A continent I never knew
But learned to love
Because "they" she said could carry
A tune
And spoke in accents never heard
In Eatonton.
Who read from *Prose and Poetry*
And loved to read "Sam McGee from Tennessee"
On nights the fire was burning low
And Christmas wrapped in angel hair
And I for one prayed for snow.

WHO IN THE FIFTIES
Knew all the written things that made
Us laugh and stories by
The hour   Waking up the story buds
Like fruit. Who walked among the flowers
And brought them inside the house
And smelled as good as they
And looked as bright.
Who made dresses, braided
Hair. Moved chairs about
Hung things from walls
Ordered baths
Frowned on wasp bites
And seemed to know the endings
Of all the tales
I had forgot.

WHO OFF INTO THE UNIVERSITY
Went exploring   To London and
To Rotterdam

Prague and to Liberia
Bringing back the news to us
Who knew none of it
But followed
crops and weather
funerals and
Methodist Homecoming;
easter speeches,
groaning church.

WHO FOUND ANOTHER WORLD
Another life   With gentlefolk
Far less trusting
And moved and moved and changed
Her name
And sounded precise
When she spoke   And frowned away
Our sloppishness.

WHO SAW US SILENT
Cursed with fear   A love burning
Inexpressible
And sent me money not for me
But for "College."
Who saw me grow through letters
The words misspelled   But not
The longing   Stretching
Growth
The tied and twisting
Tongue
Feet no longer bare

Skin no longer burnt against
The cotton.

WHO BECAME SOMEONE OVERHEAD
A light   A thousand watts
Bright and also blinding
And saw my brothers cloddish
And me destined to be
Wayward
My mother remote   My father
A wearisome farmer
With heartbreaking
Nails.

FOR MY SISTER MOLLY WHO IN THE FIFTIES
Found much
Unbearable
Who walked where few had
Understood   And sensed our
Groping after light
And saw some extinguished
And no doubt mourned.

FOR MY SISTER MOLLY WHO IN THE FIFTIES
Left us.

ELSA GIDLOW | 1898–1986

You say I am mysterious.
Let me explain myself:
In a land of oranges
I am faithful to apples.

The Nuisance

I am an inconvenient woman.
I'd be more useful as a pencil sharpener or an adding
    machine.
I do not love you the way I love Mother Jones or the
    surf coming in
or my pussycats or a good piece of steak.
I love the sun prickly on the black stubble of your cheek.
I love you wandering floppy making scarecrows of
    despair.
I love you when you are discussing changes in the class
    structure
and I'm not supposed to, and it crowds my eyes
and jams my ears and burns in the tips of my fingers.

I am an inconvenient woman.
You might trade me in on a sheepdog or a llama.
You might trade me in for a yak.
They are faithful and demand only straw.
They make good overcoats.
They never call you up on the telephone.

I love you with my arms and my legs
and my brains and my cunt and my unseemly history.
I want to tell you about when I was ten and it thundered.

I want you to kiss the crosshatched remains of my burn.
I want to read you poems about drowning myself
laid like eggs without shells at fifteen under Shelley's wings.
I want you to read my old loverletters.

I want you to want me
as directly and simply and variously
as a cup of hot coffee.
To want to, to have to, to miss what can't have room to
    happen.
I carry my love for you
around with me like my teeth
and I am starving.

Rape Poem

There is no difference between being raped
and being pushed down a flight of cement steps
except that the wounds also bleed inside.

There is no difference between being raped
and being run over by a truck
except that afterward men ask if you enjoyed it.

There is no difference between being raped
and being bit on the ankle by a rattlesnake
except that people ask if your skirt was short
and why you were out alone anyhow.

There is no difference between being raped
and going head first through a windshield
except that afterward you are afraid
not of cars
but half the human race.

The rapist is your boyfriend's brother.
He sits beside you in the movies eating popcorn.
Rape fattens on the fantasies of the normal male
like a maggot in garbage.

Fear of rape is a cold wind blowing
all of the time on a woman's hunched back.
Never to stroll alone on a sand road through pine woods,
never to climb a trail across a bald
without that aluminum in the mouth
when I see a man climbing toward me.

Never to open the door to a knock
without that razor just grazing the throat.
The fear of the dark side of hedges,
the back seat of the car, the empty house
rattling keys like a snake's warning.
The fear of the smiling man
in whose pocket is a knife.
The fear of the serious man
in whose fist is locked hatred.

All it takes to cast a rapist to be able to see your body
as jackhammer, as blowtorch, as adding-machine-gun.
All it takes is hating that body
your own, your self, your muscle that softens to flab.

All it takes is to push what you hate,
what you fear onto the soft alien flesh.
To bucket out invincible as a tank
armored with treads without senses
to possess and punish in one act,
to rip up pleasure, to murder those who dare
live in the leafy flesh open to love.

For Willyce

When i make love to you
i try
   with each stroke of my tongue
   to say
     i love you
   to tease
     i love you
   to hammer
     i love you
   to melt
     i love you

and your sounds drift down
   oh god!
   oh jesus!
     and i think
       here it is, some dude's
       getting credit for what
a woman
has done
again.

IRENA KLEPFISZ | 1941–

Death Camp

when they took us   to the shower   i saw
the rebbitzin   her sagging breasts   sparse
pubic hairs   i knew   and remembered
the old rebbe   and turned   my eyes away
i could still hear   her advice   a woman
with a husband   a scholar

when they turned   on the gas   i smelled
it   first   coming at me   pressed myself
hard to the wall   crying   rebbitzin   rebbitzin
i am here with you   and the advice you gave me
i screamed   into the wall   as the blood burst from
my lungs   cracking   her nails in women's flesh   i
     watched
her capsize   beneath me   my blood in her mouth   i
     screamed

when they dragged my body   into the oven   i burned
slowly at first   i could smell my own flesh   and could
hear   them grunt   with the weight of the rebbitzin
and they flung   her on top   of me   and i could smell
her hair burning   against my stomach

when i pressed through   the chimney
it was sunny   and clear   my smoke
was distinct   i rose quiet   left her
beneath

They Did Not Build Wings for Them

they did not build wings for them
the unmarried aunts;   instead they
crammed them into old maids' rooms
or placed them as nannies with
the younger children;   mostly they
ate in the kitchen,   but sometimes
were permitted to dine with the family
for which they were grateful and
smiled graciously as the food was passed.
they would eat slowly never filling
their plates and their hearts would
sink at the evening's end when it was
time to retreat into an upstairs corner.

but there were some who did not smile
who never wished to be grafted on
the bursting houses.   these few remained
indifferent to the family gatherings
preferring the aloneness of their small rooms
which they decorated with odd objects
found on long walks.   they collected
bird feathers and skulls unafraid to clean

them to whiteness;   stones which resembled
humped bears or the more common tiger and
wolf;   dried leaves whose brilliant colors
never faded;   pieces of wood still covered
with fresh moss and earth which retained
their moisture and continued flourishing.
these they placed by their dresser mirror
in arrangements reminiscent of secret rites
or hung over delicate watercolors of unruly
trees whose branches were about to snap
with the wind.

it happened sometimes that among these
one would venture even further.   periodically
would be heard vague tales of a woman
withdrawn and inaccessible suddenly disappearing
one autumn night leaving her room bare
of herself.   women gossiped about a man.
but eventually word would come back
she had moved north to the ocean and lived
alone.   she was still collecting
but now her house was filled with crab
and lobster shells;   discolored claws
which looked like grinning south american
parrots trapped in fish nets decorated
the walls;   skulls of unidentifiable
creatures were arranged in geometric patterns
and soft reeds in tall green bottles
lined the window sills.   one room
in the back with totally bare walls
was a workshop.   here she sorted colored

shells and pasted them on wooden boards
in the shape of common flowers.   these she sold
without sentiment.

such a one might also disappear inland.
rumor would claim she had travelled in
men's clothing.   two years later it would
be reported she had settled in the woods
on some cleared land.   she ran a small farm
mainly for supplying herself with food
and wore strangely patched dresses and shawls
of oddly matched materials.   but aloneness
was her real distinction.   the house was neat
and the pantry full.   seascapes and pastoral
scenes hung on the walls.   the garden was
well kept and the flower beds clearly defined
by color: red   yellow   blue.   in the woods
five miles from the house she had an orchard.
here she secretly grafted and crossed varieties
creating singular fruit of shades and scents
never thought possible.   her experiments rarely
failed   and each spring she waited eagerly to see
what new forms would hang from the trees.
here the world was a passionate place and she
would visit it at night baring her breasts
to the moon.

Susan's Photograph

for S.T.

I am the razor that has been put away, also
the wrist in the photograph,
and— lately— also the photographer,
the friend, the taxi, the hospital room,
the three other women, their visitors, the flowers,
and the nurse.

At the end of that summer
I started going to paramedical school
at night. Days I still talk to my students
about all the dead
overexcitable poets; all their friends;
and the living; and show the old newsreels
where they keep leaving each other, old
people, children, soldiers; and the parades:
the general, the waving people, the black horses, the black
limousines, the mules, the tall gray puppets.

But this photograph here:
a woman in a country room, in western Massachusetts,
in peace, so sad and grained:
                                        now I see you look up,
                                             outside the frame—

this room here, friends, a table, a book or two,
paper, I see you have all you need,
—even in prison you would have your childhood—

it is enough, now,
anywhere, with
everyone you love there to talk to.

FRAN WINANT | 1943–

Eat Rice Have Faith in Women

eat rice have faith in women
what I dont know now
I can still learn
if I am alone now
I will be with them later
if I am weak now
I can become strong
slowly slowly
if I learn I can teach others
if others learn first
I must believe
they will come back and teach me
they will not go away
to the country with their knowledge
and send me a letter sometime
we must study all our lives
women coming from women going to women
trying to do all we can with words
then trying to work with tools
and with our bodies
trying to stand the time it takes
reading books when there are no teachers
or they are too far away
teaching ourselves

imagining others struggling
I must believe we will be together
and build enough concern
so when I have to fight alone
there will be sisters
who would help if they knew
sisters who will come
to support me later

women demanding loyalty
each with our needs
our whole lives torn by
the old society
never given the love or work
or strength or safety or information
we could use
never helped by the institutions
that imprison us
so when we need medical care
we are butchered
when we need police
we are insulted ignored
when we need parents
we find robots
trained to keep us in our places
when we need work we are told
to become part of
the system that destroys us
when we need friends
other women tell us
I have to be selfish

youll have to forgive me
but theres only so much time
energy money concern
to go around
I have to think of myself
because who else will
I have to save things for myself
because Im not sure you could save me
if our places were reversed
because I suspect
you wont even be around
to save me when I need you . . .
Im alone on the streets
at 5 in the morning
Im alone cooking my rice
I see you getting knowledge
and having friends I dont have
and I dont see you coming back
to help me
I imagine myself getting old
I imagine I will have to go away
when Im too old to fight my way
down the streets
my friends getting younger and younger
women my age hidden in corners
in the establishment
or curled up with a few friends
isolated at home
or in the madhouse
getting their last shot of
motivation to compete

or grinding out position papers
in the movement
like old commies
waiting to be swept away
by the revolution
or in a hospital
dying of complications
nurse or nun
lesbian in clean clothes
reach out a hand to me
scientists have found
touching is necessary
and the drive to speak our needs
is basic as breath
but there isnt time
none of my needs has been met
and although Im often comfortable
this situation is painful

slowly we begin
giving back what was taken away
our right to the control of our bodies
knowledge of how to fight and build
food that nourishes
medicine that heals
songs that remind us of ourselves
and make us want to keep on with
what matters to us
lets come out again
joining women coming out
for the first time

knowing this love makes
a good difference in us
affirming a continuing life with women
we must be lovers doctors soldiers
artists mechanics farmers
all our lives
waves of women
trembling with love and anger
singing we must rage—
kissing, turn and
break the old society
without becoming the names it praises
the minds it pays

eat rice have faith in women
what I dont know now
I can still learn
slowly slowly
if I learn I can teach others
if others learn first
I must believe
they will come back and teach me

Yesterday

(*about Gertrude & Alice*)

yesterday a lovely day
we traveled to the country
bouncing along in an automobile
the sun beat directly down

feeling it on my head helps me think
we bought melons at every town
until the car was filled
ate in a small restaurant
where the fish was excellent
fed the dog under the table
we returned at evening
to sit before a fire
smelling a fire-scent found in nostrils
not in air
pleasure swells from inside
to be made visible in things
that seem less than itself
in this way life is realized
through imagination

the present moment
cannot be described
without being changed
shadings of many days
make the moment that a poem is
that is why
the butter must be tasted
and the cow seen
again and again
it takes many books to equal
one taking in and letting out
of breath

a photograph caught us
walking our dog on a cobbled street

another caught us
standing in our garden
years later we are still there
new inventions
make the moment visible
but not in the same way as poetry
here
the curve of a melon
although eliptical
can be described as
an eternal circle
in which many rounds are represented
the curve of the sky, hills
and aspects of ourselves
can thus innocently be
handled and devoured
the sun that beats directly down
is like a certain light
that spreads from your fingertips
rearranging the world
as a painted canvas does
the smoothness of the tabletop
brings you close to me
although you are lying upstairs
asleep
the grain of the wood
is the line of your eyebrows

because you are always with me
it is not true
that I go off alone to write

JUDY GRAHN | 1940–

A Woman Is Talking to Death

One
Testimony in trials that never got heard

my lovers teeth are white geese flying above me
my lovers muscles are rope ladders under my hands

we were driving home slow
my lover and I, across the long Bay Bridge,
one February midnight, when midway
over in the far left lane, I saw a strange scene:

one small young man standing by the rail,
and in the lane itself, parked straight across
as if it could stop anything, a large young
man upon a stalled motorcycle, perfectly
relaxed as if he'd stopped at a hamburger stand;
he was wearing a peacoat and levis, and
he had his head back, roaring, you
could almost hear the laugh, it
was so real.

"Look at that fool," I said, "in the
middle of the bridge like that," a very
womanly remark.

Then we heard the meaning of the noise
of metal on a concrete bridge at 50
miles an hour, and the far left lane
filled up with a big car that had a
motorcycle jammed on its front bumper, like
the whole thing would explode, the friction
sparks shot up bright orange for many feet
into the air, and the racket still sets
my teeth on edge.

When the car stopped we stopped parallel
and Wendy headed for the callbox while I
ducked across those 6 lanes like a mouse
in the bowling alley. "Are you hurt?" I said,
the middle-aged driver had the greyest black face,
 "I couldn't stop, I couldn't stop, what happened?"

Then I remembered. "Somebody," I said, "was *on*
the motorcycle." I ran back,
one block? two blocks? the space for walking
on the bridge is maybe 18 inches, whoever
engineered this arrogance, in the dark
stiff wind it seemed I would
be pushed over the rail, would fall down
screaming onto the hard surface of
the bay, but I did not, I found the tall young man
who thought he owned the bridge, now lying on
his stomach, head cradled in his broken arm.

He had glasses on, but somewhere he had lost
most of his levis, where were they?
and his shoes. Two short cuts on his buttocks,

that was the only mark except his thin white
seminal tubes were all strung out behind; no
child left *in* him; and he looked asleep.

I plucked wildly at his wrist, then put it
down; there were two long haired women
holding back the traffic just behind me
with their bare hands, the machines came
down like mad bulls, I was scared, much
more than usual, I felt easily squished
like the earthworms crawling on a busy
sidewalk after the rain; *I wanted to
leave*. And met the driver, walking back.

"The guy is dead." I gripped his hand,
the wind was going to blow us off the bridge.

"Oh my God," he said, "haven't I had enough
trouble in my life?" He raised his head,
and for a second was enraged and yelling,
at the top of the bridge—"I was just driving
home!" His head fell down. "My God, and
now I've killed somebody."

I looked down at my own peacoat and levis,
then over at the dead man's friend, who
was bawling and blubbering, what they would
call hysteria in a woman. "It isn't possible"
he wailed, but it was possible, it was
indeed, accomplished and unfeeling, snoring
in its peacoat, and without its levis on.

He died laughing: that's a fact.

I had a woman waiting for me,
in her car and in the middle of the bridge,
I'm frightened, I said.
I'm afraid, he said, stay with me,
please don't go, stay with me, be
my witness— "No," I said, "I'll be your
witness—later," and I took his name
and number, "but I can't stay with you,
I'm too frightened of the bridge, besides
I have a woman waiting
and no license—
and no tail lights—"
So I left—
as I have left so many of my lovers.

we drove home
shaking. Wendy's face greyer
than any white person's I have ever seen.
maybe he beat his wife, maybe he once
drove taxi, and raped a lover
of mine—how to know these things?
we do each other in, that's a fact.

who will be my witness?
death wastes our time with drunkenness
and depression
death, who keeps us from our
lovers.
he had a woman waiting for him,

I found out when I called the number
days later

"Where is he" she said, "he's disappeared."
He'll be all right" I said, "*we* could
have hit the guy as easy as anybody, it
wasn't anybody's fault, they'll know that,"
women so often say dumb things like that,
they teach us to be sweet and reassuring,
and say ignorant things, because we dont invent
the crime, the punishment, the bridges

that same week I looked into the mirror
and nobody was there to testify;
how clear, an unemployed queer woman
makes no witness at all,
nobody at all was there for
those two questions: what does
she do, and who is she married to?

I am the woman who stopped on the bridge
and this is the man who was there
our lovers teeth are white geese flying
above us, but we ourselves are
easily squished.

keep the women small and weak
and off the street, and off the
bridges, that's the way, brother
one day I will leave you there,
as I have left you there before,
working for death.

we found out later
what we left him to.
Six big policemen answered the call,
all white, and no child *in* them.
they put the driver up against his car
and beat the hell out of him.
What did you kill that poor kid for?
you mutherfucking nigger.
that's a fact.

Death only uses violence
when there is any kind of resistance,
the rest of the time a slow
weardown will do.

They took him to 4 different hospitals
til they got a drunk test report to fit their
case, and held him five days in jail
without a phone call.
how many lovers have we left.

there are as many contradictions to the game,
as there are players.
a woman is talking to death,
though talk is cheap, and life takes a long time
to make
right. He got a cheesy lawyer
who had him cop a plea, 15 to 20
instead of life
Did I say life?

the arrogant young man who thought he
owned the bridge, and fell asleep on it
he died laughing: that's a fact.
the driver sits out his time
off the street somewhere,
does he have the most vacant of
eyes, will he die laughing?

   Two
They don't have to lynch the women anymore

death sits on my doorstep
cleaning his revolver
death cripples my feet and sends me out
to wait for the bus alone.
then comes by driving a taxi.

the woman on our block with 6 young children
has the most vacant of eyes
death sits in her bedroom, loading
his revolver

they don't have to lynch the women
very often anymore, although
they used to—the lord and his men
went through the villages at night, beating &
killing every woman caught
outdoors.
the European witch trials took away
the independent people; two different villages
—after the trials were through that year—

had left in them, each—
one living woman:
one

What were those other women up to? had they
run over someone? stopped on the wrong bridge?
did they have teeth like
any kind of geese, or children
in them?

   Three
This woman is a lesbian be careful

In the military hospital where I worked
as a nurse's aide, the walls of the halls
were lined with howling women
waiting to deliver
or to have some parts removed.
One of the big private rooms contained
the general's wife, who needed
a wart taken off her nose.
we were instructed to give her special attention
not because of her wart or her nose
but because of her husband, the general.

as many women as men die, and that's a fact.

At work there was one friendly patient, already
claimed, a young woman burnt apart with X-ray,
she had long white tubes instead of openings;
rectum, bladder, vagina—I combed her hair, it

was my job, but she took care of me as if
nobody's touch could spoil her.

ho ho death, ho death
have you seen the twinkle in the dead woman's eye?

when you are a nurse's aide
someone suddenly notices you
and yells about the patient's bed,
and tears the sheets apart so you
can do it over, and over
while the patient waits
doubled over in her pain
for you to make the bed *again*
and no one ever looks at you,
only at what you do not do

Here, general, hold this soldier's bed pan
for a moment, hold it for a year—
then we'll promote you to making his bed.
we believe you wouldn't make such messes

if you had to clean up after them.

that's a fantasy.
this woman is a lesbian, be careful.

When I was arrested and being thrown out
of the military, the order went out: dont anybody
speak to this woman, and for those three
long months, almost nobody did: the dayroom, when

I entered it, fell silent til I had gone; they
were afraid, they knew the wind would blow
them over the rail, the cops would come,
the water would run into their lungs.
Everything I touched
was spoiled. They were my lovers, those
women, but nobody had taught us to swim.
I drowned, I took 3 or 4 others down
when I signed the confession of what we
had done   together.

No one will ever speak to me again.

I read this somewhere; I wasn't there:
in WW II the US army had invented some floating
amphibian tanks, and took them over to
the coast of Europe to unload them,
the landing ships all drawn up in a fleet,
and everybody watching. Each tank had a
crew of 6 and there were 25 tanks.
The first went down the landing planks
and sank, the second, the third, the
fourth, the fifth, the sixth went down
and sank. They weren't supposed
to sink, the engineers had
made a mistake. The crews looked around
wildly for the order to quit,
but none came, and in the sight of
thousands of men, each 6 crewmen
saluted his officers, battened down
his hatch in turn and drove into the

sea, and drowned, until all 25 tanks
were gone.   did they have vacant
eyes, die laughing, or what?   what
did they talk about, those men,
as the water came in?

was the general their lover?

   Four
A Mock Interrogation

Have you ever held hands with a woman?

Yes, many times—women about to deliver, women about to
have breasts removed, wombs removed, miscarriages,
      women
having epileptic fits, having asthma, cancer, women
      having
breast bone marrow sucked out of them by nervous or in-
different interns, women with heart condition, who were
vomiting, overdosed, depressed, drunk, lonely to the point
of extinction: women who had been run over, beaten up.
deserted, starved, women who had been bitten by rats; and
women who were happy, who were celebrating, who were
dancing with me in large circles or alone, women who
      were
climbing mountains or up and down walls, or trucks or
      roofs
and needed a boost up, or I did; women who simply
      wanted
to hold my hand because they liked me, some women who

wanted to hold my hand because they liked me better
     than
anyone.

These were many women?

Yes.   many.

What about kissing? Have you kissed any women?

I have kissed many women.

When was the first woman you kissed with serious feeling?

The first woman ever I kissed was Josie, who I had loved at
such a distance for months. Josie was not only beautiful,
she was tough and handsome too. Josie had black hair and
white teeth and strong brown muscles. Then she dropped
out of school unexplained. When she came back she came
back for one day only, to finish the term, and there was a
child in her. She was all shame, pain, and defiance. Her
     eyes
were dark as the water under a bridge and no one would
talk to her, they laughed and threw things at her. In the
afternoon I walked across the front of the class and looked
deep into Josie's eyes and I picked up her chin with my
hand, because I loved her, because nothing like her
     trouble
would ever happen to me, because I hated it that she was
pregnant and unhappy, and an outcast. We were thirteen.

You didn't kiss her?

How does it feel to be thirteen and having a baby?

You didn't actually kiss her?

Not in fact.

You have kissed other women?

Yes, many, some of the finest women I know, I have kissed.
women who were lonely, women I didn't know and didn't
want to, but kissed because that was a way to say yes we are
still alive and loveable, though separate, women who recog-
nized a loneliness in me, women who were hurt, I
     confess to
kissing the top of a 55 year old woman's head in the snow in
boston, who was hurt more deeply than I have ever been
hurt, and I wanted her as a very few people have wanted
me—I wanted her and me to own and control and run the
city we lived in, to staff the hospital I knew would mistreat
her, to drive the transportation system that had betrayed
her, to patrol the streets controlling the men who would
murder or disfigure or disrupt us, not accidently with
machines, but on purpose, because we are not allowed out
on the street alone—

Have you ever committed any indecent acts with women?

Yes, many. I am guilty of allowing suicidal women to die
before my eyes or in my ears or under my hands because I

thought I could do nothing, I am guilty of leaving a prosti-
tute who held a knife to my friend's throat to keep us from
leaving, because we would not sleep with her, we thought
she was old and fat and ugly; I am guilty of not loving her
who needed me; I regret all the women I have not slept
        with
or comforted, who pulled themselves away from me for
        lack
of something I had not the courage to fight for, for us, our
life, our planet, our city, our meat and potatoes, our love.
These are indecent acts, lacking courage, lacking a certain
fire behind the eyes, which is the symbol, the raised fist, the
sharing of resources, the resistance that tells death he will
starve for lack of the fat of us, our extra. Yes I have com-
mitted acts of indecency with women and most of them
        were
acts of omission. I regret them bitterly.

Five
Bless this day oh cat our house

"I was allowed to go
3 places, growing up," she said—
"3 places, no more.
there was a straight line from my house
to school, a straight line from my house
to church, a straight line from my house
to the corner store."
her parents thought something might happen to her.
but nothing   ever   did.

my lovers teeth are white geese flying above me
my lovers muscles are rope ladders under my hands
we are the river of life and the fat of the land
death, do you tell me I cannot touch this woman?
if we use each other up
on each other
that's a little bit less for you
a little bit less for you, ho
death, ho ho death.

Bless this day oh cat our house
help me be not such a mouse
death tells the woman to stay home
and then breaks in the window.

I read this somewhere, I wasnt there:
In feudal Europe, if a woman committed adultery
her husband would sometimes tie her
down, catch a mouse and trap it
under a cup on her bare belly, until
it gnawed itself out, now are you
afraid of mice?

   Six
Dressed as I am, a young man once called
me names in Spanish

a woman who talks to death
is a dirty traitor

inside a hamburger joint and
dressed as I am, a young man once called me

names in Spanish
then he called me queer and slugged me.
first I thought the ceiling had fallen down
but there was the counterman making a ham
sandwich, and there was I spread out on his
counter.

For God's sake I said when
I could talk, this guy is beating me up
can't you call the police or something,
can't you stop him? he looked up from
working on his sandwich, which was *my*
sandwich, I had ordered it. He liked
the way I looked. "There's a pay phone
right across the street" he said.

I couldn't listen to the Spanish language
for weeks afterward, without feeling the
most murderous of urges, the simple
association or one thing to another,
so damned simple.

The next day I went to the police station
to become an outraged citizen
Six big policemen stood in the hall,
all white and dressed as they do
they were well pleased with my story, pleased
at what had gotten beat out of me, so
I left them laughing, went home fast
and locked my door.
For several nights I fantasized the scene
again, this time grabbing a chair

and smashing it over the bastard's head,
killing him. I called him a spic, and
killed him. My face healed, his didnt
no child *in* me.

now when I remember I think:
maybe *he* was Josie's baby.
all the chickens come home to roost,
all of them.

   Seven
Death and disfiguration

One Christmas eve my lovers and I
we left the bar, driving home slow
there was a woman lying in the snow
by the side of the road. She was wearing
a bathrobe and no shoes, where were
her shoes? she had turned the snow
pink, under her feet, she was an Asian
woman, didnt speak much English, but
she said a taxi driver beat her up
and raped her, throwing her out of his
car.
what on earth was she doing there
on a street she helped to pay for
but doesn't own?
doesn't she know to stay home?

I am a pervert, therefore I've learned
to keep my hands to myself in public
but I was so drunk that night,

I actually did something loving
I took her in my arms, this woman,
until she could breathe right, and
my friends who are perverts too
they touched her too
we all touched her.
"You're going to be all right"
we lied. She started to cry
"I'm 55 years old" she said
and that said everything.

Six big policemen answered the call
no child *in* them.
they seemed afraid to touch her,
then grabbed her like a corpse and heaved her
on their metal stretcher into the van,
crashing and clumsy.
She was more frightened than before.
they were cold and bored.
'don't leave me' she said.
'she'll be all right' they said.
we left, as we have left all of our lovers
as all lovers leave all lovers
much too soon to get the real loving done.

  Eight
a mock interogation

Why did you get into the cab with him, dressed as you are?

I wanted to go somewhere.

Did you know what the cab driver might do
if you got into the cab with him?

I just wanted to go somewhere.

How many times did you
get into the cab with him?

I dont remember.

If you dont remember, how do you know it happened to
    you?

  Nine
Hey you death

ho and ho poor death
our lovers teeth are white geese flying above us
our lovers muscles are rope ladders under our hands
even though no women   yet go down to the sea in ships
except in their dreams.

only the arrogant invent a quick and meaningful end
for themselves, of their own choosing.
everyone else knows how very slow it happens
how the woman's existence bleeds out her years,
how the child shoots up at ten and is arrested and old
how the man carries a murderous shell within him
and passes it on.

we are the fat of the land, and
we all have our list of casualties

to my lovers I bequeath
the rest of my life

I want nothing left of me for you, ho death
except some fertilizer
for the next batch of us
who do not hold hands with you
who do not embrace you
who try not to work for you
or sacrifice themselves or trust
or believe you, ho ignorant
death, how do you know
we happened to you?

wherever our meat hangs on our own bones
for our own use
your pot is so empty
death, ho death
you shall be poor

DIANE DI PRIMA | 1934–

Annunciation

the tall man, towering,
it seemed to me
in anger. I was fifteen only
& his urgency
(murderous rage) an assault I
bent under. I saw the lilies bend
also.   I had been spinning
flax: violet for the temple veil. I had just
gone to the well for water & when I returned
he was there. A flat stone. Towering.
                    Murderous rage
like the Law. They call it
love. His voice
was harsh,   I bent,   I tried to
evade.
Sound trembled in my gut, my
bowels
spoke w/ fear—
                    the red tiles
shifted beneath me; a light
flashed from his eyes, his hand, the blue stone
in his ring & my bowels caught
w/ fear. He said
    "HAIL, FULL OF GRACE" I remember

my hand
found a psalter, something real, the smooth vellum
sunwarmed
under my fingers
the wind had stilled, the lilies
bent of themselves, my body
bent under weight of robes
white muslin gleamed in my tears
                              in sunlight
like a gold brocade
& my head too bent
under weight of hair. I fell
to my knees, I salted
the ground before me

He did not move, his voice
had turned to thunder, there was
no word to remember.   but Womb
        He spoke of my womb.
        The fruit of my womb.
Sunlight & thunder. I had not
        heard thunder before
        in such blinding light.

———

the rose, the thorn, the thistle
the rose, the thorn, the myrtle
the lily, the thorn, the thistle
the lily & the myrtle
the lily, the rose, the thistle
the lily, the thistle, the myrtle

—————

The wind
bent the palm trees again
the room was empty

I stood again, as one stands
        after earthquake
my young girl's hands
began to spin the scarlet thread
        for the temple

KATHLEEN FRASER | 1937–

The History of My Feeling

for D.

The history of my feeling for you (or is it the way you
                                      change
and are blameless like clouds)
                reminds me of the sky in Portland
and the morning I unpacked
and found the white plates from Iowa City
broken,
      consistently surprising with cracks,
petals like new math theories smashed
           with the purposeful fingers of chance.
I loved the plates. They were remnants from an auction
which still goes on in my head because of the auctioneer's
           body
and his sexy insinuations about the goods he was selling.

But to Ruth, who talked them into their thin wraps of
           newspaper,
what we were sharing was departure and two lives
           breaking
and learning
      to mend into new forms.

We had loved our husbands,
                    torn our bodies in classic ways to bear
                        children: Sammy, David, Wesley—
Now we loved new men and wept together
so that the plates weren't important and hadn't been
                                                packed
with the care I might have given had I been alone.
But Ruth was with me.

You were gone, like this storm that's been arriving and
                                        disappearing
all morning.
                I awoke to hear heavy rain in the gutters.
The light was uncertain and my feelings had grown less
                                                sure.
Last night, pinned by a shaft of pain—
                your presence and your absence—
I knew clearly that I hated you
for entering me profoundly, for taking me inside you,
for husbanding me, claiming all that I knew
                        and did not know,
yet letting me go from you
into this unpredictable and loneliest of weathers.

Semele Recycled

After you left me forever,
I was broken into pieces,
and all the pieces flung into the river.
Then the legs crawled ashore
and aimlessly wandered, the dusty cow-track.
They became, for a while, a simple roadside shrine:
A tiny table set up between the thighs
held a dusty candle, weed-and-fieldflower chains
placed reverently there by children and old women.
My knees were hung with tin triangular medals
to cure all forms of hysterical disease.

After I died forever in the river,
my torso floated, bloated in the stream,
catching on logs or stones among the eddies.
White water foamed around it, then dislodged it;
after a whirlwind trip, it bumped ashore.
A grizzled old man who scavenged along the banks
had already rescued my arms and put them by,
knowing everything has its uses, sooner or later.

When he found my torso, he called it his canoe,
and, using my arms as paddles,
he rowed me up and down the scummy river.

When catfish nibbled my fingers he scooped them up
and blessed his reusable bait.
Clumsy but serviceable, that canoe!
The trail of blood that was its wake
attracted the carp and eels, and the river turtle,
easily landed, dazed by my tasty red.

A young lad found my head among the rushes
and placed it on a dry stone.
He carefully combed my hair with a bit of shell
and set small offerings before it
which the birds and rats obligingly stole at night,
so it seemed I ate.
And the breeze wound through my mouth and empty
      sockets
so my lungs would sigh, and my dead tongue mutter.
Attached to my throat like a sacred necklace
was a circlet of small snails.
Soon the villagers came to consult my oracular head
with its waterweed crown.
Seers found occupation, interpreting sighs,
and their papyrus rolls accumulated.

Meanwhile, young boys retrieved my eyes
they used for marbles in a simple game
till somebody's pretty sister snatched at them
and set them, for luck, in her bridal diadem.
Poor girl! When her future groom caught sight of her,
all eyes, he crossed himself in horror,
and stumbled away in haste
through her dowered meadows.

What then of my heart and organs,
my sacred slit
which loved you best of all?
They were caught in a fisherman's net
and tossed at night into a pen for swine.
But they shone so by moonlight that the sows stampeded,
trampled one another in fear, to get away.
And the fisherman's wife, who had thirteen living children
and was contemptuous of holy love,
raked the rest of me onto the compost heap.

Then in their various places and helpful functions,
the altar, oracle, offal, canoe and oars
learned the wild rumor of your return.
The altar leapt up, and ran to the canoe,
scattering candle grease and wilted grasses.
Arms sprang to their sockets, blind hands with nibbled nails
groped their way, aided by loud lamentation,
to the bed of the bride, snatched up those unlucky eyes
from her discarded veil and diadem,
and rammed them home. Oh, what a bright day it was!
This empty body danced on the riverbank.
Hollow, it called and searched among the fields
for those parts that steamed and simmered in the sun,
and never would have found them.

But then your great voice rang out under the skies
my name!—and all those private names
for the parts and places that had loved you best.
And they stirred in their nest of hay and dung.
The distraught old ladies chasing their lost altar,

and the seers pursuing my skull, their lost employment,
and the tumbling boys, who wanted the magic marbles,
and the runaway groom, and the fisherman's thirteen
    children
set up such a clamor, with their cries of "Miracle!"
that our two bodies met like a thunderclap
in midday—right at the corner of that wretched field
with its broken fenceposts and startled, skinny cattle.
We fell in a heap on the compost heap
and all our loving parts made love at once,
while the bystanders cheered and prayed and hid their eyes
and then went decently about their business.

And here it is, moonlight again; we've bathed in the river
and are sweet and wholesome once more.
We kneel side by side in the sand;
we worship each other in whispers.
But the inner parts remember fermenting hay,
the comfortable odor of dung, the animal incense,
and passion, its bloody labor,
its birth and rebirth and decay.

Gesture

It is a gesture I do
that grew
out of my mother
in me.

I am trying to remember
what she
was afraid to say
all those

years, fingers folded
against her mouth,
head turned away.

AUDRE LORDE | 1934–1992

To My Daughter
the Junkie on a Train

Children we have not borne
bedevil us by becoming
themselves
painfully sharp   unavoidable
like a needle in our flesh.

Coming home on the subway from a PTA meeting
of minds committed to murder   or suicide
in their own private struggle
a long-legged girl with a horse in her brain
slumps down beside me
begging to be ridden asleep
for the price of a midnight train
free from desire.

Little girl   on the nod
if we are measured by dreams we avoid
then you are the nightmare
of all sleeping mothers
rocking back and forth
the dead weight of your arms
locked about our necks
heavier than our habit
of looking for reasons.

My corrupt concern will not replace
what you once needed
but I am locked into my own addiction
and offer you my help   one eye
out for my own station.

Roused and deprived
your costly dream explodes
in terrible technicolored laughter
at my failure
up and down   across the aisle
women avert their eyes
as other mothers who became useless
curse our children   who became junk.

A Litany for Survival

For those of us who live at the shoreline
standing upon the constant edges of decision
crucial and alone
for those of us who cannot indulge
the passing dreams of choice
who love in doorways coming and going
in the hours between dawns
looking inward and outward
at once before and after
seeking a now that can breed
futures
like bread in our children's mouths
so their dreams will not reflect
the death of ours;

For those of us
who were imprinted with fear
like a faint line in the center of our foreheads
learning to be afraid with our mother's milk
for by this weapon
this illusion of some safety to be found
the heavy-footed hoped to silence us
For all of us
this instant and this triumph
We were never meant to survive.

And when the sun rises we are afraid
it might not remain
when the sun sets we are afraid
it might not rise in the morning
when our stomachs are full we are afraid
of indigestion
when our stomachs are empty we are afraid
we may never eat again
when we are loved we are afraid
love will vanish
when we are alone we are afraid
love will never return
and when we speak we are afraid
our words will not be heard
nor welcomed
but when we are silent
we are still afraid.

So it is better to speak
remembering
we were never meant to survive.

A Poem for Women in Rage

A killing summer heat wraps up the city
emptied of all who are not bound to stay
a black woman waits for a white woman
leans against the railing in the Upper Westside street
at intermission
the distant sounds of Broadway dim to lulling
until I can hear the voice of sparrows
like a promise I await
the woman I love
our slice of time
a place beyond the city's pain.

In the corner phonebooth a woman
glassed in by reflections of the street between us
her white face dangles
a tapestry of disasters seen
through a veneer of order
her mouth drawn like an ill-used roadmap
to eyes without core, a bottled heart
impeccable credentials of old pain.

The veneer cracks open
hate hunches through the glaze into my afternoon
our eyes touch like hot wire
and the street snaps into nightmare
a woman with white eyes is clutching
a bottle of Fleischmann's gin
is fumbling at her waistband
is pulling a butcher knife from her ragged pants
her hand arcs backward "You Black Bitch!"

the heavy blade spins out toward me
slow motion
years of fury surge upward like a wall
I do not hear it
clatter to the pavement at my feet.

A gear of ancient nightmare churns
swift in familiar dread and silence
but this time I am awake, released
I smile. Now. This time is
my turn.
I bend to the knife my ears blood-drumming
across the street my lover's voice
the only moving sound within white heat
"Don't touch it!"
I straighten, weaken, then start down again
hungry for resolution
simple as anger and so close at hand
my fingers reach for the familiar blade
the known grip of wood against my palm
I have held it to the whetstone
a thousand nights for this
escorting fury through my sleep
like a cherished friend
to wake in the stink of rage
beside the sleep-white face of love

The keen steel of a dreamt knife
sparks honed from the whetted edge with a tortured
        shriek
between my lover's voice and the grey spinning

a choice of pain or fury
slashing across judgment like a crimson scar
I could open her up to my anger
with a point sharpened upon love,

In the deathland my lover's voice
fades
like the roar of a train derailed
on the other side of a river
every white woman's face I love
and distrust is upon it
eating green grapes from a paper bag
marking yellow exam-books tucked into a manilla folder
orderly as the last thought before death
I throw the switch.
Through screams of crumpled steel
I search the wreckage for a ticket of hatred
my lover's voice
calling
a knife at her throat.

In this steaming aisle of the dead
I am weeping
to learn the names of those streets
my feet have worn thin with running
and why they will never serve me
nor ever lead me home.
"Don't touch it!" she cries
I straighten myself
in confusion
a drunken woman is running away

down the Westside street
my lover's voice moves me
to a shadowy clearing.

Corralled in fantasy
the woman with white eyes has vanished
to become her own nightmare
a french butcher blade hangs in my house
love's token
I remember this knife
it carved its message into my sleeping
she only read its warning
written upon my face.

Elegy

for Janis Joplin

Crying from exile, I
mourn you, dead singer, crooning and palming
your cold cheeks, calling you: You.
A man told me you died; he was
foreign, I felt for the first time, drunk, in his car, my
throat choked: You won't sing for me
now. Later I laughed in the hair between
his shoulder-blades, well enough
loved in a narrow
bed; it was
your Southern Comfort
grin stretching my
mouth. You were in me
all night,

shouting our pain, sucking off
the mike, telling a strong-headed
woman's daily beads to dumb kids
creaming on your high
notes. Some morning at wolf-hour
they'll know.
Stay in my
gut, woman lover I never

touched, tongued, or sang to; stay
in back of my
throat, sandpaper
velvet, Janis, you
overpaid your
dues, damn it, why are you dead?

Cough up your whisky gut
demon, send him home howling
to Texas, to every
fat bristle-chinned
white motel keeper on
Route 66, every half-
Seminole waitress with a
crane's neck, lantern-jawed
truck driver missing a
finger joint, dirt-farmer's
blond boy with asthma and sea dreams,
twenty-one-year-old
mother of three who got far
as Albuquerque once.

Your veins were
highways from
Coca-Cola flatland,
dust and dead
flies crusting the
car window till it rained.
Drive! anywhere
out of here, the
ratty upholstery smelling

of dogpiss and cunt,
bald tires swiveled and
lurched on slicked macadam
skidding the funk in your mouth
to a black woman's tongue.

Faggots and groupies and
meth heads loved you, you
loved bodies and booze
and hard work, and more
than that, fame. On your
left tit was a tattooed
valentine, around your
wrist a tattooed filigree; around
your honeycomb brain webbed
klieg lights and amp circuits screamed
Love Love and the booze-
skag-and-cocaine baby twisted your
box, kicked your
throat and the songs came.

I wanted to write your
blues, Janis, and put my
tongue in your mouth that way.
Lazy and grasping and
treacherous, beautiful
insomniac freaking the ceiling,
the cold smog went slowly blue, the cars
caught up with your heartbeat, maybe you were not
alone, but the ceiling told you
otherwise, and skag said:

You are more famous than anyone
out of West Texas, your hair is a
monument, your voice preserved
in honey, I love you, lie down.

I am in London and
you, more meat than Hollywood
swallowed, in Hollywood, more
meat. You got me through
long nights with your coalscuttle
panic, don't be scared
to scream when it hurts
and oh mother it hurts, tonight
we are twenty-seven, we are
alone, you are dead.

Poem: On Declining Values

In the shadows of the waiting room
are other shadows
beaten
elderly women or
oldfolk bums
depending on your point of view

but
all depending

formerly mothers formerly wives
formerly citizens of some acceptable
position
but
depending and
depending

now exposed unable and unwashed
a slow and feeble crawling through the city
varicose
veins bulging
while the arteries the intake systems
harden
wither

shrivel
close
depending and depending

II

She will leave Grand Central Station
and
depending
spend two hours in St. Patrick's
if the guards there
if police ignore the grovelling length
of time it takes
a hungry woman
just to pray

but here
she whispers
with an aging boyfriend
fugitive and darkblue suited out
for begging who
has promised her a piece
of candy or an orange or an apple
if
they meet tomorrow
if the cops don't chase them separated
wandering under thin
gray hair

III

meanwhile
cops come quick
knockbopping up the oakwood benches
BANG
BOP
"GET OUTAHERE," they shout around
the ladies women sisters dying old and all
the formerly wives and mothers
shuffle soft
away
with paper shopping bags beside them

almost empty

and a medium young man
comes up
to ask a question:
"Tell me, I mean, seriously,
how does it feel to be beautiful?"

And I look back at him
a little bit alarmed
a little bit amused
before I say:

"It all depends too much
on you."

Roman Poem Number Six

You walk downstairs
to see this man who moves so
quietly in a dark room
where there are balancing
scales on every table.
Signore D'Ettore can tell
you anything about
communications if you mean
the weight the price
of letters
packages
and special post cards.
Hunch-back
short
his grey hair always groomed
meticulous
with a comb and just a touch
of grease
       for three months
he has worn the same well
tailored suit
a grey suit quite unlike
his hair.
      I find it restful
just to watch him making
judgements all of us accept.
"But are you sad?", he asks
me looking up.
"The world is beautiful

but men are bad," he says in
slow Italian.
I smile with him but still the problem
is not solved.
The photographs of Rome
must reach my father but the big
official looking book seems blank
the finger-nail of Signore D'Ettore
seems blind and wandering
from line to line among the countries
of a long
small-printed list.
"Jamaica? Where is Jamaica?"
I am silent. My Italian
is not good enough to say, "Jamaica
is an island where you can find
calypso roses sunlight and an old man
my father
on his knees."

Case in Point

A friend of mine who raised six daughters and
who never wrote what she regards as serious
until she
was fifty-three
tells me there is no silence peculiar
to the female

I have decided I have something to say
about female silence: so to speak
these are my 2¢ on the subject:
2 weeks ago I was raped for the second
time in my life the first occasion
being a whiteman and the most recent
situation being a blackman actually
head of the local NAACP

2

Today is 2 weeks after the fact
of that man straddling
his knees either side of my chest
his hairy arm and powerful left hand
forcing my arms and my hands over my head
flat to the pillow while he rammed
what he described as his quote big dick
unquote into my mouth
and shouted out: "D'ya want to swallow
my big dick; well, do ya?"

He was being rhetorical.
My silence was peculiar
to the female.

Living Alone (I)

In this silvery now of living alone,
doesn't it seem, I ponder,
anything can happen?
On the flat roof of a factory
at eye level from my window,
starling naiads dip in tremulous rainpools
where the sky floats, and is no smaller
than long ago.
Any strange staircase, as if I were twenty-one—
any hand drawing me up it,
could lead me to my life.
Some days.

And if I coast, down toward home, spring evenings,
    silently,
a kind of song rising in me to encompass
Davis Square and the all-night
cafeteria and the pool hall,
it is childhood's song, surely no note is changed,
sung in Valentines Park or on steep streets in the map of
    my mind
in the hush of suppertime, everyone gone indoors.
Solitude within multitude seduced me early.

Living Alone (II)

Some days, though,
living alone,
there's only knowledge of silence,
clutter of bells cobwebbed
in crumbling belfry,
words jaggéd,
in midutterance broken.

Starlings, as before,
whistle wondering at themselves,
crescendo, diminuendo.
My heart pounds away,
confident as a clock.
Yet there is silence.

New leafed, the neighbor trees
round out. There's one,
near my window,
seems to have no buds, though.

Epilogue

I thought I had found a swan
but it was a migrating snow-goose.

I thought I was linked invisibly to another's life
but I found myself more alone with him than without
   him.

I thought I had found a fire
but it was the play of light on bright stones.

I thought I was wounded to the core
but I was only bruised.

Rhyme of My Inheritance

My mother gave me a bitter tongue.
My father gave me a turned back.
My grandmother showed me her burned hands.
My brother showed me a difficult book.
These were their gifts; the rest was talk.

I discovered my body in the dark.
It had a surprise in its little crack.
I started to say what I'd found in the dark,
but my mother gave me a dirty look
and my father turned a key in the lock.

I was left alone with the difficult book
and the stove that burned my grandmother's hands,
and while they muttered behind my back
I learned to read and to make my bread,
to eat my words and lie flat in my bed.

They took me to school where I learned to be cute:
I wore clean jumpers and washed my hands;
I put my hands up to cover my mouth;
I listened to everything everyone said
and kept what I could in my stuffed-up head.

I had weeping eyes and a chest that coughed,
a stomach that hurt, and a mouth that laughed
whether or not I felt good or bad.
I was always promoted to the next grade.
I graduated; I got laid.

I did what girls were supposed to do.
I wore a white dress; I was photographed;
my teeth were perfect, my knees were crossed.
I cleaned up the mess that the baby made.
I hope that my body's price is paid.

I'm giving the gifts back, one by one.
I'm tearing the pages of my past.
I'm turning my back. I'm turning them down.
I'm burning their strict house to the ground.
May I never want bread at their table again.

May I let go of these bitter rhymes;
and may this burial be my last
while I live in my body and learn from my bones
to make some less predictable sound.
Let this coffin of verses inherit my pain.

Song

for female voices

Suddenly nothing is coming right.
My lovely child has become fat.
Her face is red with ugly scabs.
Love, does it mean I am a bad

       Mummy, please stay with me.
       Don't go to work today.
       My tummy hurts. I want
       milk in my bottle. I want

mother? I wanted to be a great
authoress. Or author's mistress—
I am always late to work. Always
I wanted to be a perfect woman,

       you to lie down with me.
       I peed again in bed—
       my daddy never yells.
       Now you're making me cry.

a mother, big, with wonderful dinners
in the pot, and children I only sing to,
a woman woven of different threads:
flat in the kitchen, but in bed

       I only want my daddy.
       Can't he take care of me?
       He calls me his little
       baby and tucks me in.

I'll play a lute of long hair
and little nightgown; I'll move
like a soft-coated animal; the moon
will be drawn to touch my body in love.

> I want my blanket. Please,
> can't we go to the zoo?
> When I'm big I'll get real babies.
> Then I'll be just like you.

Some Unsaid Things

I was not going to say
how you lay with me

nor where your hands went
& left their light impressions

nor whose face was white
as a splash of moonlight

nor who spilled the wine
nor whose blood stained the sheet

nor which one of us wept
to set the dark bed rocking

nor what you took me for
nor what I took you for

nor how your fingertips
in me were roots

light roots torn leaves put down—
nor what you tore from me

nor what confusion came
of our twin names

nor will I say whose body
opened, sucked, whispered

like the ocean, unbalancing
what had seemed a safe position

LOUISE GLÜCK | 1943–

Pomegranate

First he gave me
his heart. It was
red fruit containing
many seeds, the skin
leathery, unlikely.
I preferred
to starve, bearing
out my training.
Then he said Behold
how the world looks, minding
your mother. I
peered under his arm:
What had she done
with color & odor?
Whereupon he said Now *there*
is a woman who loves
with a vengeance, adding
Consider she is in her element:
the trees turning to her, whole
villages going under
although in hell
the bushes are still
burning with pomegranates.
At which

he cut one open & began
to suck. When he looked up at last
it was to say My dear
you are your own
woman, finally, but examine
this grief your mother
parades over our heads
remembering
that she is one to whom
these depths were not offered.

Dedication to Hunger

I   FROM THE SUBURBS

They cross the yard
and at the back door
the mother sees with pleasure
how alike they are, father and daughter—
I know something of that time.
The little girl purposefully
swinging her arms, laughing
her stark laugh:

It should be kept secret, that sound.
It means she's realized
that he never touches her.
She is a child; he could touch her
if he wanted to.

2 GRANDMOTHER

"Often I would stand at the window—
your grandfather
was a young man then—
waiting, in the early evening."

That is what marriage is.
I watch the tiny figure
changing to a man
as he moves toward her,
the last light rings in his hair.
I do not question
their happiness. And he rushes in
with his young man's hunger,
so proud to have taught her that:
his kiss would have been
clearly tender—

Of course, of course. Except
it might as well have been
his hand over her mouth.

3 EROS

To be male, always
to go to women
and be taken back
into the pierced flesh:

        I suppose
memory is stirred.

And the girl child
who wills herself
into her father's arms
likewise loved him
second. Nor is she told
what need to express.
There is a look one sees,
the mouth somehow desperate—

Because the bond
cannot be proven.

4   THE DEVIATION

It begins quietly
in certain female children:
the fear of death, taking as its form
dedication to hunger,
because a woman's body
is a grave; it will accept
anything. I remember
lying in bed at night
touching the soft, digressive breasts,
touching, at fifteen,
the interfering flesh
that I would sacrifice
until the limbs were free
of blossom and subterfuge: I felt
what I feel now, aligning these words—
it is the same need to perfect,
of which death is the mere byproduct.

5   SACRED OBJECTS

Today in the field I saw
the hard, active buds of the dogwood
and wanted, as we say, to capture them,
to make them eternal. That is the premise
of renunciation: the child,
having no self to speak of,
comes to life in denial—

I stood apart in that achievement,
in that power to expose
the underlying body, like a god
for whose deed
there is no parallel in the natural world.

BERNADETTE MAYER | 1945–

Eve of Easter

Milton, who made his illiterate daughters
Read to him in five languages
Till they heard the news he would marry again
And said they would rather hear he was dead
Milton who turns even Paradise Lost
Into an autobiography, I have three
Babies tonight, all three are sleeping:
Rachel the great great great granddaughter
Of Herman Melville is asleep on the bed
Sophia and Marie are sleeping
Sophia namesake of the wives
Of Lewis Freedson the scholar and Nathaniel
     Hawthorne
Marie my mother's oldest name, these three girls
Resting in the dark, I made the lucent dark
I stole images from Milton to cure opacous gloom
To render the room an orb beneath this raucous
Moon of March, eclipsed only in daylight
Heavy breathing baby bodies
Daughters and descendants in the presence of
The great ones, Milton and Melville and Hawthorne,
     everyone is speaking
At once, I only looked at them all blended
Each half Semitic, of a race always at war

The rest of their inherited grace
From among Nordics, Germans and English,
    writers at peace
Rushing warring Jews into democracy when actually
Peace is at the window begging entrance
With the hordes in the midst of air
Too cold for this time of year,
Eve of Easter and the shocking resurrection idea
Some one baby stirs now, hungry for an egg
It's the Melville baby, going to make a fuss
The Melville one's sucking her fingers for solace
She makes a squealing noise
Hawthorne baby's still deeply asleep
The one like my mother's out like a light
The Melville one though the smallest wants the most
Because she doesn't really live here
Hawthorne will want to be nursed when she gets up
Melville sucked a bit and dozed back off
Now Hawthorne is moving around, she's the most hungry
Yet perhaps the most seduced by darkness in the room
I can hear Hawthorne, I know she's awake now
But will she stir, disturbing the placid sleep
Of Melville and insisting on waking us all
Meanwhile the rest of the people of Lenox
Drive up and down the street
Now Hawthorne wants to eat
They all see the light by which I write, Hawthorne sighs
The house is quiet, I hear Melville's toy
I've never changed the diaper of a boy
I think I'll go get Hawthorne and nurse her for the
    pleasure

Of cutting through darkness before her measured noise
Stimulates the boys, I'll cook a fish
Retain poise in the presence
Of heady descendants, stone-willed their fathers
Look at me and drink ink
I return a look to all the daughters and I wink
Eve of Easter, I've inherited this
Peaceful sleep of the children of men
Rachel, Sophia, Marie and again me
Bernadette, all heart I live, all head, all eye, all ear
I lost the prejudice of paradise
And wound up caring for the babies of these guys

HONOR MOORE | 1945–

Polemic #1

This is the poem to say "Write poems, women" because I want to
   read them, because for too long, we have had mostly men's lives
      or men's imaginations wandering through
  our lives, because even the women's lives we have details of
come through a male approval desire filter which diffuses
      imagination, that most free part of ourselves.
One friend is so caught on the male-approval-desire hook she
   can't even write a letter. Ink on paper would be clear
      evidence of failure to be Sylvia
   Plath or Doris Lessing, or (in secret) William ButlerYeats.
Hilda Doolittle, the poet who hid behind "H.D.," splashed
      herself with ink just before writing to make her
feel free, indifferent toward the mere means of writing. I would take
   ink baths if I'd be splashed free of male approval desire.
      This male-approval-desire filter and its
    attached hook, abbreviated M-A-D filter and hook,
have driven many women mad, could drive me mad, won't because
      I see all the other women fighting the M
Male A Approval D Desire, and I clench my fists to hold
   their hands, and I am not as alone as my grandmother
      was who painted, was free and talented and
    who for some M-A-D reason married, had kids, went mad and
      stopped finishing her paintings at thirty-five.
M-A-D is the filter through which we're pressed to see ourselves—
   if we don't, we won't get published, sold, or exhibited—
      I blame none of us for not challenging it

except not challenging it may drive us mad. It is present
in the bravest of us. It comes out in strange shapes, escapes
      like air through the tiniest hole in the strongest
woman's self. It is a slaughterhouse waiting for the calf
   or lamb-sized art, for the sausage-ready little pig poems
      which never get to the supermarket: They
   are lost in the shuffle, or buried as ladies' poems have been
in bureau drawers for years. Male Approval Desire is a cog
      in the Art Delivery Machine: It instructs
by quiet magic women to sing proper pliant tunes for
   father, lover, piper who says he has the secret, but
      wants ours; it teaches us to wear cloaks labelled
   Guinevere, become damsels, objects in men's power joustings
like her: lets us shimmer, disappear, promise to rise like a
      Lady of the Lake, but we drown—real, not phantom.
The Art Delivery Machine is ninety-nine and forty-
   four hundredths percent pure male sensibility, part of
      a money system ninety-nine and forty-
   four hundredths percent pure white-male-power-structure
                        controlled. So
you may wonder why I write this poem and say "Write your
                        own poems,
      women!" Won't we be crushed trying? No. We have more
now, fifty-six hundredths percent of the Art Delivery
   Machine. We can't be stopped. So I write this polemic I
      call a poem, say "Write poems, women." I want to
   read them. I have seen you watching, holding on and
                        watching, and
I see your lips moving. You have stories to tell, strong stories;
   I want to hear your minds as well as hold your hands.

First Time: 1950

In the back bedroom, laughing when you pull
something fawn-colored from your black
tight pants, the unzipped chino slit.
I keep myself looking at the big belt
buckled right at my eyes, feel the hand
riffle my hair: You are called Mouse, baby-

sitter trusted Wednesdays with my baby
brother. With me. I still see you pull
that huge bunch of keys from a pocket, hand
them to my brother, hear squeaking out back—
Mrs. Fitz's clothesline—as you unbelt,
turn me to you, my face to the open slit.

It's your skin, this thing, head, its tiny slit
like the closed eye of a still-forming baby.
As you stroke, it stiffens like a new belt—
your face gets almost sick. I want to pull
away, but you grip my arm. I see by your black
eyes you won't let go. With your left hand

you take my chin. With your other hand
you guide it, head reddening, into my slit,
my five-year-old mouth. In the tight black
quiet of my shut eyes, I hear my baby
brother shaking the keys. You lurch, pull
at my hair. I don't breathe, feel buckle, belt,

pant. It tastes lemony, musty as a belt
after a day of sweat. Mouth hurts, my hands
push at your hips. I gag. You let me pull
free. I open my eyes, see the strange slits
yours are; you don't look at me. "Babe, babee—"
You are moaning, almost crying. The black

makes your skin clam-white now, your jewel-black
eyes blacker. You buckle up the thick belt.
When you take back the keys, my baby
brother cries. You extend a shaking hand
you make kind. In daylight through a wide slit
an open shade leaves, I see her pull,

Mrs. Fitz pulling in her rusty, soot-black
line. Framed by a slit, her window, her large hands
flash, sort belts, dresses, shirts, baby clothes.

MARTHA COURTOT | 1941–2000

i am a woman in ice
melting

piece by piece
slowly
i am divested
of the cold cage

sharp as glass
the splinters fall at my feet
do not cut yourself

when i listen
to the trains wail
i can feel
through underground caverns
of stalactal promises

the earth
full and steady
under me
move

i never thought
i'd love the sun again
but now my fingers move
in a panic
of wanting to be burnt

After Touch

after late evenings
filled with women

after talk
or touch

after a song by janis joplin
and a woman's body in my arms
quite by accident, swaying
and slowly stepping in a dance
like those dances of high school
back at the dawn of sex

after kissing my friends
a safe goodbye at the door

after the long ride
underground/under mind
and the transfer, the platform
desolate and calm
with waiting men
lounging in seats
or closing their eyes, free,
free to doze
or accost me as they please

and the cab ride or terror
five blocks home from the station

after hot showers, hot chocolate
and books

I lie down in bed
beside the dark shape of a man
thinking of women

awake

not wanting masturbation
that old ploy
my clitoris fooled,
rubbed, drugged, bribed
into submission
when it's my whole body,
woman-hungering, aches

i remember now a childhood story
of a man of the last century
who drove a team of horses
forty miles through a blizzard
to bring back wheat
for his starving midwestern town

and how, when he lived,
when at last he lay down
in his own safe bed
his fingers, itching and burning,

his tingling feet
kept him awake all night

and he was glad. the pain
meant they would thaw, meant
he would dance, chop wood,
hold wagon reins again

i am a lesbian

ANNE WALDMAN | 1945–

Lady Tactics

she,
   not to be confused with she, a dog
               she, not to be confused with she, Liberty
       she a waif
            she a wastrel
                  she, a little birdie
she, not to be confused with pliable
          she in plethora
                  she in blue
she with the pliers, or behind the plough
       she
          not to be confused with a jonquil
she in the imperative
           she the liveliest of creatures
      she, not to be confused with Pandora or plaintiff
          or getting seasick or prim
she, a prima donna
           she a secret she a dreamer
she in full force, she rushing home
      she at a desk or in a book
        she, not to be confused with she, a secretary
she a goddess
          she, not to be confused with the Slovak
      she recuperating

she, not to be confused with mutton
she a muse
she on a mission, not languishing
she in the landscape, she in silk
she, not to be confused with juniper
with jodhpurs
she with idiosyncrasies
she in labor
she, not to be confused with the
conifer
she in consanguinity
she at long last
she, wind, sea, Pompeii, deliberation, home
she in middle C
she the sharpest
she, obliged
she in distinguished sentiments
not to be confused with sentimental
or sly

OLGA BROUMAS | 1949–

Caritas

Thank someone for being
that one. Walk with her
to the center of a place
and back again
singing a little song.
Burn something.
                    SENECA

1

Eric Satie, accused
once of formlessness, composed
a sonata titled: Composition In The Form
Of A Pear. When I tell you
that it would take
more brilliance than Mozart
more melancholy precision than Brahms
to compose a sonata in the form of
your breasts, you
don't believe me. I lie
next to your infidel sleep, all night
in pain
and lonely with my silenced
pleasure. Your breasts
in their moonlit pallor
invade me, lightly, like minor
fugues. I lie

between your sappling thighs, my tongue
flat on your double lips, giving
voice, giving
voice. Opulent
as a continent in the rising light, you sleep
on, indifferent
to my gushing praises.
Is as it should be. Atlantis,
Cyprus, Crete, the encircled
civilizations, serene
in their tidal basins, dolphin-
loved, didn't heed to the faint, the
riotous
praise
of the lapping sea.

2

Your knees, those pinnacles
competing with the finest
dimpled, five-
year-old chins are
dancing. Ecstatic as nuns
in their delirious habit, like
runaway needles on a multiple graph,
the first organic model of
seismographs, charting
the crest I keep you on
and on till all
the sensitive numbers on the
Richter scale ring out at
once, but

silently: a choir
of sundial alarums. You reach that place,
levitated by pleasure, the first
glimpse the melting
glacier must
have had, rounding the precipice
of what came to be known as
Niagara Falls. After all this time,
every time,
like a finger inside
the tight-gummed,
spittle-bright, attavistic
suckle of
a newborn s fragile-lipped
mouth, I
embrace you, my heart
a four celled embryo, swimming
a pulse, a bloodstream that becomes, month
to month, less
of a stranger's, more
intimate, her
own.

3

There are people who do not explore the in-
Sides of flowers . . .
    Sandra Hochman

With the clear
plastic speculum, transparent
and when inserted, pink like the convex
carapace of a prawn, flashlight in hand, I

guide you
inside the small
cathedral of my cunt. The unexpected
light dazzles you. This flesh, my darling, always
invisible like the wet
side of stones, the hidden
hemisphere of the moon, startles you
with its brilliance, the little
dome a spitting
miniature of the Haghia Sophia
with its circlet of openings
to the Mediterranean Sun.
A woman-made language would
have as many synonyms for pink/light-filled/holy as
the Eskimo does
for snow. Speechless, you
shift the flashlight from
hand to hand, flickering. An orgy
of candles. Lourdes in mid-August. A flurry of
audible breaths, a seething
of holiness, and
behold
a tear
forms in the single eye, carmine
and catholic. You too, my darling, are
folded, clean
round a light-filled temple, complete
with miraculous icon, shedding
her perfect tears, in touch
with the hidden hemispheres
the dome
of our cyclops moon.

She's white and her shoulders sing
like a singular vein of marble
alive and kicking in the jagged hill.
Her eyes are wet heaps
of seaweed in the sullen dusk.
Eyes of shadow and latitudes. Eyes of slate
eyes of flint, eyes the color of certain stones
prized above all by Georgia
O'Keeffe. Eyes of an agile
wilderness, wings of a desert
moth. Her handsome hands. Each
one a Duchess in her splendid gardens, each
one a pastry cook at her pliable dough, each one
a midwife at her palpable labor, the referee
of our relay race.
Her belly lulls me like an immense coastline
of dunes beneath a floating gull.
Her belly lulls me in a lustrous bowl
so precious
all the Asiatic dynasties   .
roll in their gilded graves, tarnished
with envy. Skin like the awning of
a ceremonial tent, the cloth draped over
the bread and wine of
an ungodly marriage. *Is not this love
also a tavern? Is this meal not also
a public meal?* I am encircled like a pit
in the fruit's ripe stomach, an ovum in cilia-lined
amniotic space, a drunken satellite, home
at last from its dizzy orbit.

Strike
up the music, my
love will dance. The loaf
of bread held against her breasts, the blade
in her nimble fingers, her feet stamping patterns
like snakes in the circle of dust, her waist a
scorpion's, she'll
dance, dance
the bread dance, slicing
out flawless ovals from
her inexhaustible loaf.

5

Imagine
something so beautiful
your liver would swell with contraband
chemicals, laughter, the dangerous
and infectious song.
Something so fine
you'd need no alibi for
your avid enchantment. A small
thing to start with: a special hairline
on a special nape, bent
low towards you. Imagine now
how your fingertips throb. You follow
the spinal valley, dipping
its hollow core like a ladle of light
in your ministering fingers.
Intuit the face
like that of a woman's
inscribed upon the porous

tablets of the law, rich with an age,
with tenderness, various, and like a map
of recurring lives. Here the remnants of
an indefatigable anger, the jubilant
birthyell, here the indelible
covens of pleasure, a web
of murmurs, a lace
mantilla of sighs.
Recapture
the fleshy mouth full of fissures, the tongue
on the sated lip, the residual flare
of a regal nostril, the purple shade
of an earlobe, the eyebrows meeting
squarely above the lids.
You laugh
at this like a daughter, a young
sprig of amaranth caught
in your gelding teeth, that fade-
less flower you call a pigweed, a prince's
feather, a love-
lies-bleeding. But
not this love. Laugh, lover, laugh
with me. In that side-
splitting reservoir, in the promised calm
of its heaving waters, you'll
bend, you'll see this woman's
beautiful
and familiar face.

Eugene, December 1976

CAROLYN FORCHÉ | 1950–

Burning the Tomato Worms

That from which these things are born
That by which they live
That to which they return at death
Try to know that

    I

Now pines lift
Linking their dark spines
Weak clouds fly the breaks like pelicans
                        over ploughed land
During thick fields of American wind
Between apples and the first snow
In horse-breath weather I remember her

    2

Before I was born, my body as snowfat
Crept over Wakhan
As grandfathers spat into fires and thawed
Their tarpaulin
Sending crackled paths of blood
Down into my birth

Their few logs were sleeves of fire
Twists of smoke still brush
Out of the ice where they died

3

Anna's hands were like wheat rolls
Shelling snow peas, Anna's hands
Are both dead, they were Uzbek,
Uzbek hands known for weaving fine rugs

Eat Bread and Salt and Speak the Truth

She was asking me to go with her
To the confrontation of something
That was sacred and eternal
It was a timeless, timeless thing
Nothing of her old age or my childhood
Came between us

4

Her footsteps bloodied snow
Smoke from her bread fire crept
From the house
The wood grew white in her stove

When time come
We go quick
I think
What to take

On her back ground wheat and straw dolls
In the sack white cheese, duck blood

Mother of God
I tell you this
Dushenka
You work your life
You have nothing

5

I came down from her in south Michigan
Picture the resemblance

Now I squint out over the same fields scraped in sun
And now I burn tomato worms and string useless gourds

She had drawn apple skin
Tightly bent feet
Pulled babushkas and rosary beads
On which she paid for all of us

She knew how much grease
How deep to seed
That cukes were crawlers

Every morning at five she would market
Or wake me to pick and hoe, crows
Cackling between us, Slovakia swear words
Whenever I stopped to feed them

This is the way we have it
Light a glass of candles
Heavy sweatered winter woman
Buried the October before I was grown

6

She would take gladiolas to the priest
Like sword sprouts they fumed near her bed

After raising my father and nine others
In a foreign country
Find yourself a good man
Get married
There is nothing left

Before we have a village
Across the Slovakian border
Now
There is no Slovakia

Before we dance like gypsies
Listen
You—young yet

7

Still the china Virgin
Plugs in below the mantelpiece, lights up
Pointing at her own heart
Big as a fist and full of daggers

I get down on my knees with every other Slavic woman
And we speak the language

8

She took up against her hoe stick, watched the moon
She could hear snow touch chopped wood

Her room smelled of advent candles
Cake flour clung to her face

9

Between apples and first snow
In horse-breath weather
Birds shape the wind
Dogs chained to the ground
Leave their dung
Where the ditches have burned

And I wish she were alive
But she is big under the ground, dead
I walk to the Eastern market
A half block under October suns that move away
Women still there selling summer squash
But always more die

10

Moons fill with blood nights
Crab-walking northeast
My father has left the garden
To seed, first frost
We lug tomatoes in worms and all

11

Stiff air, same color as a child's vein
Rigid against the freezing curls of birch bark
The snow's round thaw at fence-post bases
Snow deep across the yard
Ice grunting with boot heels

And a small sun an inch across like blood
On the frost when some trap
Chomps down a rabbit whose dark eyes
Wait for dogs

12

I chew up my gloves on the way to the barn
I wait in the pony stall for a boy
To come, circle his tongue
In my mouth while the stud horse
Muds floorboards beside us

Bales of feed split beneath
Our bellies, we wait like nothing
For tires to grind past beside us
Over a new fall in the road

All day snapping knives to the back side of the shed
He waits for me
Winter light spreading out in our houses
His own father downing a shot of Four Roses
Playing songs on combs and kleenex

When you hear them hoot owls hollerin'
It's a sign a rain

13

I want to ask you why I live
And we go back apart across the field
Why I am here and will have to feel the way I die

It was all over my face
Grandma flipped kolačy rolls
Dunked her hands in bowls of water
Looked at me
Wrung the rags into the stoop
Kept it from me
Whatever she saw

ALICE NOTLEY | 1945–

A California Girlhood

The Brothers Grimm grew weaker and flickered, blue light
    in the well. Hans Christian Andersen
and his tiny gossamer bride went to bed beneath a walnut
                              shell
    encrusted with every star, Copenhagen's
Sky, dreamed Louisa May Alcott, but when we awaken
    in New England my head will rest on
my cousin's shoulder, beneath *my* tree.
Anna Sewell, that the shining aren't suffered to continue to
    shine! though, old, he finds
his way home, Carolyn Keene's blue roadster
    cannot replace the young horse. There's nothing
left of her, Michael Shayne, but lipstick and
    fingerprints on a cognac bottle; Erle Stanley Gardner
knows the Chief will never pass cross-examination
    and on to ripeness, the breasts!
Where is orphan Canada, Anne of Green Gables?
    the smell of a white dress it rained on because
it was graduation. Frank G. Slaughter
    has given him hands that heal her after
she sleeps through rape by a snob. Frank Yerby
    pierces right through the membrane she cries
out triumphantly, one of the others, skim
    bunches of adjectives.
Margaret Mitchell moved to the eye which
    watered 3 times: that bright moon moves on. But

you can't strain hydrogen and oxygen out of tears
     or Raphael Sabatini out of life, Captain
Blood, the sword is worn
     against my tattered petticoat.
Charlotte Brontë is tense and comely as a first child.
Emily Brontë walks out to copulate with a
     storm. Indigo to emerald to
indigo, the Mississippi "better den rum darlin"; then
     Mark Twain gets hit on the hammer
and glowers a whole other lifetime. Anya
Seton sighed. "If only angels be angels and witchery
     the fine art it is
                    I still have to
bother about something besides décolletage."
Gwen Bristow pulled the arrow out of her arm
     and thrust it into the Indian's chest.
When a guy goes molten John Dickson Carr
     orders the witch is nonexistent, yawn
Sigrid Undset loses her life and yet loses nothing
     as a river in her bed flows beneath
the stained-glass leaves, thy breath is sustenance.
She wouldn't rollerskate through the Swedish palace,
     Annamarie Selinko. Lawrence Schoonover
respects the first man to use a fork in Spain,
     a Jew of Inquisition times,
she dances in little but castanets, Kathleen
     Windsor, it's a scheming pussy wind
that ripples and funs with the bleak sea. Knowledge
     of evil an inadequate knowledge, as
Herman Melville would say, read National
     Geographic, for your first glimpse of nipples,

free maps, Arctic, Hibiscus. Jane Austen
    sneaks a suspicion. You look like the
flash with the cash.
    John Steinbeck. My name
                        is Rose o'Sharon
the gorgeous coarse prayer, as the sentimental horrors
encroach and recede, repeatedly. Edgar Allan Poe
is on purple alert. Alexander Dumas, fils, announces
My favorite song is Rainy Night in Georgia.
Daphne DuMaurier wept tiny drops of Dom Perignon. Did
    Lady Brett Ashley copulate? did
Herman Wouk read between the lines?
T. H. White allowed one her manhood; Guinevere is
    Jenny, but I know I carry a lance.
William Faulkner incomprehensible, an
    obsidian cliff, does the ballerina wear cleats?
She puts her ear to the delicate shell of Ernest
    Hemingway; hears
Willa Cather orchestrate her death. Victoria Holt
    is still, chastely, dandy in love.

The Goddess Who Created
This Passing World

The Goddess who created this passing world
Said Let there be lightbulbs & liquefaction
Life spilled out onto the street, colors whirled
Cars & the variously shod feet were born
And the past & future & I born too
Light as airmail paper away she flew
To Annapurna or Mt. McKinley
Or both but instantly
Clarified, composed, forever was I
Meant by her to recognize a painting
As beautiful or a movie stunning
And to adore the finitude of words
And understand as surfaces my dreams
Know the eye the organ of affection
And depths to be inflections
of her voice & wrist & smile

MAUREEN OWEN | 1943–

She had ruby red lacquer on her fingernails
sprinkled with gold glitter
elbow to wrist tin bracelets
a skinny shimmy-down   baby blue gown
of velvet portiere with peaked shoulders
trimmed in squirrel
gilded thongs crisscrossed around each lavender ankle
Her hair in the numerous tight braids
Of the Saharan girls   hung with
dried seeds and etched copper ornaments
with impeccable minute triangular boxes   engraved
and stained   hinges like the jaws
of some marvelous microscopic fish
under a broad-brimmed European hat   of
beaded Zulu designs   A plump skin pouch
A piece of flawless quartz at her throat
She was at least six feet tall strapped on her platforms
standing on the corner of 108th St.
in front of a heavenly azure wall   with a cloud sign
saying   PARIS BLUES

"Wanting You"

While you were going   up the hill   in the
stunning snow   the dazzling crystals that
floated & fell   in the streetlights
Snug inside your black 1930s coat,   images
of your   "Goodbye   Goodbye"   rehearsed vivaciously
in my mind   a sudden cynosure where my attention
knelt in rapt admiration   So made with love!
So frantic with desire!   Again and again I watch
you turn before me   That slightly inclining
three-quarter turn   Your gloved hand poised
the overwhelming irresponsible joy of your voice
as it stepped into the gay Russian Troika   the
stamping   steaming horses!   the gold & blue banners!
My heart left me then   tumbling & splashing up
the hill   the snow melting where it touched

Waking up alone   I explode from the bed
nervous & shaking   in this steamy room
It is these moments that have led me here
this need I have to sleep beside you
that has caused all the trouble in my life.

Honesty

Honesty is all right for men, but I don't
think it does a woman any good at all.

JANA HARRIS | 1947–

Don't Cheapen Yourself

You look sleazy tonight
ma said.
Cheap, I said
I'm doin cheap.
You got any idea
how much it costs
to do cheap these days?
To do gold City of Paris
three-inch platform sandals
and this I. Magnin snake dress?
I'm doin cheap.
You look like a bird, she said
a Halloween bird with red waxed lips.
    —In high school
you could either do cheap or Shakespeare,
college prep or a pointy bra,
ratting a bubble haircut
with a toilet brush.
I was not allowed to do high school cheap;
I did blazers and wool skirts
from the Junior League thrift shop.
In high school it was
don't walk in the middle of
Richie, Leelee, and the baby,

you might come between them.
You look like a skag
wearin that black-eyed makeup,   .
people are gunna think you're cheap.
While I poured red food dye
on my hair
to match my filly's tail for the rodeo,
ma beat her head against the wall,
she said
tryin to make me nice.
I tried real hard,
but the loggers, the Navy guys,
they always hit on me.
Cause you're an easy mark, ma said.
And I played guilty,
I played guilty every time.
But now, I said
now I'm doin cheap.

RAE ARMANTROUT | 1947–

Anti-Short Story

A girl is running. *Don't* tell me
"She's running for her bus."

All that aside!

Tone

1

Hoping my face shows the pleasure I felt, I'm
smiling languidly. Acting. To put your mind
at rest—how odd! At first we loved because
we startled one another

2

     Not pleased to see the
     rubberband, chopstick, tin-
     foil, this pen, things
     made for our use

     But the bouquet you made of
     doorknobs, long nails for
     their stems   sometimes
     brings happiness

3

Is it bourgeois to dwell on nuance? Or effeminate?
Or should we attend to it the way a careful animal
sniffs the wind?

4

Say the tone of an afternoon

Kindly but sad

"The ark of the ache of it"

12 doorsteps per block

5

In the suburbs butterflies
still spiral up the breeze
like a drawing of weightlessness.
To enter into this spirit!
But Mama's saying she's alright
"as far as breathing and all that"

6

When you're late I turn slavish, listen hard for
your footstep. Sound that represents the end of
lack

FANNY HOWE | 1940–

The Nursery

The baby
    was made in a cell
in the silver & rose underworld.
Invisibly prisoned
    in vessels & cords, no gold
for a baby; instead
eyes, and a sudden soul, twelve weeks
old, which widened its will.

Tucked in the notch of my fossil: bones
    laddered a spine from a cave,
the knees & skull
were etched in this cell, no stone, no gold
where no sun brushed its air.

One in one, we slept together
    all sculpture
        of two figures welded.
But the infant's fingers
squeezed & kneaded
        me, as if to show
the Lord won't crush what moves
on its own . . . secretly.

On Robeson Street
        anonymous
was best, where babies
have small hearts
        to learn
with;
    like intimate
thoughts on sea
water, they're limited.

Soldered to my self
   it might be a soldier or a thief
for all I know.
The line between revolution & crime
  is all in the mind
     where ideas of righteousness
and rights confuse.
I walked the nursery floor.
By four-eyed buttons & the curdle of a cradle's
paint: a trellis of old gold
    roses, lipped & caked
where feet will be kicking in wool.

      Then the running,
the race after,
cleaning the streets up for a life.
His technicolor cord
hung from a gallery of bones,
    but breathing *I'm finished*.
Both of us.

And when the baby sighed,
through his circle of lips,
                    I kissed it,
        and so did he, my circle to his,
we kissed ourselves and each other,
        as if each cell was a Cupid,
and we were born to it.

The cornerstone's dust
upfloating

by trucks & tanks.
White flowers spackle

the sky crossing the sea.
A plane above the patio

wakes the silence
and my infant who raises

his arms to see
what he's made of.

O animation! O liberty!

TOI DERRICOTTE | 1941–

In Knowledge of Young Boys

i knew you before you had a mother,
when you were newtlike, swimming,
a horrible brain in water.
i knew you when your connections
belonged only to yourself,
when you had no history
to hook on to,
barnacle,
when you had no sustenance of metal
when you had no boat to travel
when you stayed in the same
place, treading the question;
i knew you when you were all
eyes and a cocktail,
blank as the sky of a mind,
a root, neither ground nor placental;
not yet
red with the cut nor astonished
by pain, one terrible eye
open in the center of your head
to night, turning, and the stars
blinked like a cat. we swam
in the last trickle of champagne

before we knew breastmilk—we
shared the night of the closet,
the parasitic
closing on our thumbprint,
we were smudged in a yellow book.

son, we were oak without
mouth, uncut, we were
brave before memory.

MICHELLE CLIFF | 1946–

Women's Work

I

The breastmilk of a scrubwoman mixes with the darkening water in a galvanized tin bucket—spreads with the suds across the floor—mingles with the residue of daytime residents—tracked in.

Between chairlegs she moves—pushes aside heavy oaken desks—crawling across black and white tiles she reaches the toilets. This is Chicago—the early part of this century.

At five a.m. the chill seeps into her wet dress as she waits to go home.

In Jamaica in the 1820s a slavewoman is found with roots and leaves she has gathered—arranged around her: slowly pounding the elements together in a hollowed-out calabash. She is preparing a solution.

In her cabin at night a blackwoman chooses abortion. But she is caught—her penalty: an iron collar to be worn until her child is born.

Glasgow 1856.
Back against a quieted loom, the spinner shifts—
then shuts her eyes against the hands of the supervisor—

submits—
her own hands grasp the frame—
plait a pattern in the dangling threads—
left over from another woman's shift:
an artwork of necessity.

On a postcard a row of blackwomen stand—
trackwomen of the B&O—
with shovels ready to dig a railroad bed.
It is wartime and manpower is short.
These women range in age—and dress—
yet all wear slacks.
They leave behind kitchens—not just their own.
Children—not just their own.
And rows and rows of other people's land.

They are here for the "duration."

An abbess in fifteenth-century Bologna decides on strict
rules for closure. Heavy curtains divide the nuns from
those who visit—and no one may lodge within.

The abbess dies. The nuns exhume her body—seat her in
a chapel they build themselves—and decorate the walls
with her paintings.

And worship her.

They report this all to the bishop—
saying her fingertips are still pink.

The abalone fisherwoman stands in her wet red cloth—
her knife held in her teeth—full basket—her friend
kneels alongside.

And in New York Sakiko Ide:
knife held against chrysanthemum—
slicing the bloom in two.

In Malaysia in an electronics factory a woman sees a
spirit in her microscope—another woman's face. Along
the line she alerts the other workers—there is excite-
ment: their mothers' likenesses have come to disrupt
production.

The owners call this a "subconscious wildcat strike."

France 1590.
A woman is laboring in fire.
The child emerges between her legs.
Flames lick and sear their flesh.
Looking down she sees what she has done:
"another witch the less."

India 1979. Satyrani Chadha finds her daughter; the
bulge of the child is not apparent: "There were no eyes,
no mouth . . . it was just a twisted black bundle lying
in a corner . . . the mother-in-law . . . told me to pick
up my rubbish and clear her courtyard."

I built these images of knowledge—
of remains.
of burying grounds.

> Of Quemadero de la Cruz where scholars thought
> they had discovered a new geological strata
> running the length of a city and looked closer
> and found teeth and hair and fat and bits of cloth
> mixed in—welded together.

Ravensbrück combines with Troy.

of belladonna: clean cloths.

> Julia Stephen advising a tender preparation
>   of the dead.
> Assata Shakur demanding to birth herself.
> Florence Nightingale draining wounds,
> Ethel Rosenberg cradling a prostitute
>   at the Women's House of Detention.

of forces underground.

> Harriet Tubman with her gun.
> Susan B. Anthony with her gun.
> Burns removed by boiling white vinegar
>   in the pan.
> Whispered instructions—
> the radical rose with its black center.

But also:

> The mother-in-law burning
> the daughter-in-law:
> while the son has a glass of milk.

The stakes in the square one afternoon in Augsburg
were so thick it seemed to be a forest: We are still
learning to recognize what we see.

Traces erased. Details removed.
Letters sewn into quilts—or burned.
Self-portraits hidden in trunks—or burned.

The perishable nature of so many of our artifacts.

Shrines erected over shrines.
The line replaces the circle.

If we do these things to remember witches
If in our remembrance we find the depth of our history
Will we opt for description only
or choose to ignite the fuse of our knowledge?

III

"Whales Lure Scientists with Their Friendliness"—the
headline reads. Gray whales are traveling south. We see
them from the car—their sweet skins surface side by
side. Slick with wetness—streaked white from salt. They
carry barnacles—responsible for life outside, as well as
life within.

We are two women traveling south. And court these
female pairs.

There's a need for romance in this work.

We are two women traveling over backroads one evening. Past the farm which raises Arabian stallions. We will be apart soon and need this evening. Your hand rests lightly on my leg—"go slower," you ask. I pull off the road to let the pick-up bearing down pass us.

On a dirt road now, I glance back. Two cars are parked at its mouth. The road becomes a cow-path. I turn. Headlights glare. The cars are in front and behind us. "Hey, honey, want some?" a driver yells—

I reason: gang-rape. I reason: maybe guns.
I spin the car wheels. Somehow get out.
It is that quick.

There's a need for rage in this work.

RACHEL BLAU DuPLESSIS | 1941–

Nessie

for Woolf

She was a great
fury   a great furry   sleek black otter
seal with a snaky decor.   Long writhing writing
along her coiling.

People paralyzed on their verandas,
"It is she!"   She!   not a snake   a giant
black   sleek   never seen before   she had shown only
a small part
before.

Maddened,   longing,   crying,   with open doggy mouth
she threw herself again and again against the window
her wrinkled working face

will she get in?   she slid into the room   no one knew
        what.
They had never recognized   never wanted to?
they were wondering.

JANE MILLER | 1949–

Many Junipers, Heartbeats

The river wasn't cold.
As we swam, I imagined a sonata
with some clouds in the background.

I believed some of it.
To put it into words,
she was the metaphor of a girl.

I would not have known
how to manage my body
if she asked me.

The surface sprawled like a sheet,
and on it I wept for her.
Over the veil which sleeps between women

I wept, and over the sad schoolboy
irrevocably destined for her.
She prayed without opening her lips.

She was cognac, she was frangipani.
They told me finally to stop
my soliciting. How could I have ever

considered her carried away by sentiment—
wore her inconsolable customs
which chill women and rivers at the source.

Under the Zanzariere

She put the comb in one hand and with the left waved.
With that deliberate ambivalence I've come to hate. The
slow kiss which lands on my face like a wasp. It began in
childhood. Mother desired her and they spent hours
together. If not in the garden surrounded by dahlias
and clover, inside the musty hallways or under the
zanzariere.

They very deliberately excluded others, though I should
say they were kind to me. When they bathed I listened,
not to their laughter which in itself was omnivorous, but
to the splashing, the pauses. I had too much respect for
Mother to be surprised. For example, her choice of
linden flowers for the bath.

They went on like this, conspicuous in the dark. They
would brush each other's long heavy hair. Mother was
terribly young, but not at all innocent, as you must
realize. Once, on the terrace, a liana plant straining
toward light amused them. She let Claire eat its flowers.

The thought of them upstairs in their horribly white chamber, with late afternoon light, disgusted me. I began to study insects, collecting their persistent voices, like whispers in another room.

SHARON OLDS | 1942–

Satan Says

I am locked in a little cedar box
with a picture of shepherds pasted onto
the central panel between carvings.
The box stands on curved legs.
It has a gold, heart-shaped lock
and no key. I am trying to write my
way out of the closed box
redolent of cedar. Satan
comes to me in the locked box
and says, *I'll get you out. Say*
My father is a shit. I say
my father is a shit and Satan
laughs and says, *It's opening.*
Say your mother is a pimp.
My mother is a pimp. Something
opens and breaks when I say that.
My spine uncurls in the cedar box
like the pink back of the ballerina pin
with a ruby eye, resting beside me on
satin in the cedar box.
Say shit, say death, say fuck the father,
Satan says, down my ear.
The pain of the locked past buzzes
in the child's box on her bureau, under

the terrible round pond eye
etched around with roses, where
self-loathing gazed at sorrow.
Shit. Death. Fuck the father.
Something opens. Satan says
Don't you feel a lot better?
Light seems to break on the delicate
edelweiss pin, carved in two
colors of wood. I love him too,
you know, I say to Satan dark
in the locked box. I love them but
I'm trying to say what happened to us
in the lost past. *Of course*, he says
and smiles, *of course. Now say: torture.*
I see, through blackness soaked in cedar,
the edge of a large hinge open.
*Say: the father's cock, the mother's
cunt*, says Satan, *I'll get you out.*
The angle of the hinge widens
until I see the outlines of
the time before I was, when they were
locked in the bed. When I say
the magic words, Cock, Cunt,
Satan softly says, *Come out.*
But the air around the opening
is heavy and thick as hot smoke.
Come in, he says, and I feel his voice
breathing from the opening.
The exit is through Satan's mouth.
Come in my mouth, he says, *you're there
already*, and the huge hinge

begins to close. Oh no, I loved
them, too, I brace
my body tight
in the cedar house.
Satan sucks himself out the keyhole.
I'm left locked in the box, he seals
the heart-shaped lock with the wax of his tongue.
It's your coffin now, Satan says.
I hardly hear;
I am warming my cold
hands at the dancer's
ruby eye—
the fire, the suddenly discovered knowledge of love.

Coral Sea, 1945

for My Mother

My mother is walking down a path
to the beach.
She has loosened her robe,
a blood-colored peignoir,
her belly freed
from the soft restraint of silk.
In a week I will be born.

Out on a reef
a small fleet waits for the end of the world.
My mother is not afraid.
She stares at the ships,
the lifting mask of coral,
and thinks: *the world is ending*.
The sea still orchid-colored before her
and to the south the ships in their same formation

but now the reef extends itself,
the sea thrusts up its odd red branches
each bearing a skeletal blossom.
I have no desire to be born.

In the coral sea
the parrots sing in their bamboo cages
the pearls string themselves in the mouths of the oysters
it snows inside the volcano

but no one believes these things.

And these things are not believable:
not the reef feeding itself
nor the ships moving suddenly, in formation.

Nor my body burning inside hers
in the coral sea
near the reef of her lungs

where I hung in the month of December.
In the year the war ended
the world opened,
ending for me
with each slow tremor
cold
invisible as snow
falling
inside the volcano.

Among Women

What women wander?
Not many. All. A few.
Most would, now & then,
& no wonder.
Some, and I'm one,
Wander sitting still.
My small grandmother
Bought from every peddler
Less for the ribbons and lace
Than for their scent
Of sleep where you will,
Walk out when you want, choose
Your bread and your company.

She warned me, "Have nothing to lose."

She looked fragile but had
High blood, runner's ankles,
Could endure, endure.
She loved her rooted garden, her
Grand children, her once
Wild once young man.
Women wander
As best they can.

MOLLY PEACOCK | 1947–

She Lays

She lays each beautifully mooned index finger
in the furrow on the right and on the left
sides of her clitoris and lets them linger
in their swollen cribs until the wish to see the shaft
exposed lets her move her fingers at the same time
to the right and left sides pinning back
the labia in a nest of hair, the pink sack
of folds exposed, the purplish ridge she'll climb,
when she lets one hand re-pin the labia
to free the other to wander with a withheld
purpose as if it were lost in the sands when the Via
To The City appeared suddenly, exposed:
when the whole exhausted mons is finally held
by both hands is when the Via gates are closed,

but they are open now, as open as her
thighs lying open among the arranged pillows.
Secrets have no place in the orchid boat of her
body and old pink brain beneath the willows.
This is self-love, assured, and this is lost time.
This is knowing, knowing, known
since growing, growing, grown;
revelation without astonishment,
understanding what is meant.
This is world-love. This is lost I'm.

KATHA POLLITT | 1949–

Metaphors of Women

What if the moon
was never a beautiful woman?
Call it a shark shearing across black water.
An ear. A drum in a desert.
A window. A bone shoe.

What if the sea
was discovered to have no womb?
Let it be clouds, blue as the day they were born.
A ceremony of bells and questions.
A toothache. A lost twin.

What if a woman
is not the moon or the sea?
Say map of the air. Say green parabola.
Lichen and the stone that feeds it.
No rain. Rain.

JANE COOPER | 1924–2007

The Green Notebook

There are 64 panes in each window of the Harrisville
    church
where we sit listening to a late Haydn quartet. Near the
    ceiling clouds
build up, slowly brightening, then disperse, till the
    evening sky
glistens like the pink inside of a shell over uncropped grass,
over a few slant graves.

At Sargent Pond the hollows are the color of strong tea.
Looking down you can see decomposed weeds and the
    muscular bronze and green
stems of some water lilies. Out there on the float
three figures hang between water and air, the heat
    breathes them, they no longer speak.
It is a seamless July afternoon.

Nameless. Slowly gathering. . . . It seems I am on the
    edge
of discovering the green notebook containing all the
    poems of my life,
I mean the ones I never wrote. The meadow turns
    intensely green.
The notebook is under my fingers. I read. My
    companions read.
Now thunder joins in, scurry of leaves. . . .

San Sepolcro

In this blue light
    I can take you there,
snow having made me
    a world of bone
seen through to. This
    is my house,

my section of Etruscan
    wall, my neighbor's
lemontrees, and, just below
    the lower church,
the airplane factory.
    A rooster

crows all day from mist
    outside the walls.
There's milk on the air,
    ice on the oily
lemonskins. How clean
    the mind is,

holy grave. It is this girl
    by Piero

della Francesca, unbuttoning
    her blue dress,
her mantle of weather,
    to go into

labor. Come, we can go in.
    It is before
the birth of god. No one
    has risen yet
to the museums, to the assembly
    line—bodies

and wings—to the open air
    market. This is
what the living do: go in.
    It's a long way.
And the dress keeps opening
    from eternity

to privacy, quickening.
    Inside, at the heart,
is tragedy, the present moment
    forever stillborn,
but going in, each breath
    is a button

coming undone, something terribly
    nimble-fingered
finding all of the stops.

Unleashed

Candida took me to Fiorucci on Friday.
She encouraged me to buy the poster of the woman
I fell in love with. She is blondish, stepping
Out of the ocean with a very knowing boyish
Look in her eye, lovely thin arms, nice breasts
And her mid-section is flat tanned and softly
Muscular. I just couldn't buy a poster
Of a woman in Fiorucci—"Lookit the big dyke buyin
A poster of a chick." She's on my wall right now,
Always stepping out of the ocean and I like her
Very much. Candida just said "Buy it."
Even Barbara after a while admitted she was okay.
We sat on the couch sipping Lite beer discussing
The woman's body and I wonder if she drinks beer.
I'll meet her some night in Amsterdam. She'll have
These big boots on and she'll be sipping a Heineken's.
I'll remind her of the poster and she'll say: "Oh that."
Barbara came visiting New York two years ago and I
Came in smoking a cigar and that's how she remembers
Me. I saw this woman with beautiful sad eyes
In Rose's loft. She puts up posters on the wall of
Veiled women from Iran, and then she writes
Lesbian Nation on the kitchen wall and she changes
     everything.

Barbara comes in the door in a pure white teeshirt and
Brand new Lees. "He told me to come back at ten." "I'm
Writing a poem." "Go ahead." Apples banana and orange
In the bowl left over from lunch. Barbara's nipples
    standing
Up in her white teeshirt—some guy on twenty-third street
Said "I like your titties" to Barbara and I kicked him
In the leg. I think I scared myself more than him.
Barbara's lying on the bed reading a book. I don't
Know where this is going at all, getting wider and wider.
I'm running into the next room in the bar in Amsterdam:
"Barbara, she's here, the Fiorucci woman . . . Barbara,
    Barbara."

Joan

Today, May 30th, Joan
of Arc was burned.
She was 19 and
when she died
a man saw white doves
fly from her mouth.

Joan was born in 1512
between Lorraine
and Champagne. Joan
was raised on legends.
Merlin said France would be
lost by a woman and saved

by a virgin. Joan was
not an adventurous girl, not
a tomboy, but very dreamy,
good, stay-at-home,
the baby of the family.
Joan never got her period.

She heard these voices
in the bells, she saw angels
in colored glass. She believed
the sun moved around
the earth because that's
what she saw. She believed
God wanted Charles VII
to be King of France
because that's what Michael,
Catherine & Margaret told
her when she listened to
the bells. Her father
said he'd drown her
if she didn't stop this
nonsense.

She was 19 years old
when they burned her body in the middle of town
while she was still alive. A white dove
came out of her mouth as she died.
Four hundred and thirty-one years ago today.
A dove leaped right out of her mouth.

BIOGRAPHICAL NOTES

SOURCES AND ACKNOWLEDGMENTS

INDEX OF POETS, TITLES,
AND FIRST LINES

BIOGRAPHICAL NOTES

ALTA (Alta Gerrey; b. 1942) founded Shameless Hussy Press in Oakland in 1969. Among the first feminist presses in America, it published books by writers such as Susan Griffin, Pat Parker, and Ntozake Shange, as well as alta's own collections *Letters to Women* (1970) and *No Visible Means of Support* (1972). A collected edition of her writings, *The Shameless Hussy: Selected Stories, Essays, & Poetry*, was published in 1980. She currently owns an art gallery in Berkeley.

RAE ARMANTROUT (b. 1947) was born in Vallejo, California, educated at Berkeley and San Francisco State, and now teaches in the Literature Department at University of California, San Diego. She has gathered her poetry in *Extremities* (1978), *The Invention of Hunger* (1979), *Precedence* (1985), *Couverture* (1991), *Necromance* (1991), *Made To Seem* (1995), *Veil: New and Selected Poems* (2001), *The Pretext* (2001), *Up to Speed* (2004), and *Next Life* (2007), and she has also published a memoir, *True* (1998).

OLGA BROUMAS (b. 1949) was born in Hermoupolis, Greece, and immigrated to the U.S. in 1967; she published her first book of poems in her native language, and has translated the works of Greek poet Odysseas Elytis. Since 1990, she has been poet-in-residence at Brandeis University, where she also directs the creative writing program. Her books include *Beginning with O* (1977), *Soie Sauvage* (1980), *Pastoral Jazz* (1983), *Black Holes, Black Stockings* (1985, with Jane Miller), *Perpetua* (1989), and *Rave: Poems, 1975–1999* (1999).

RITA MAE BROWN (b. 1944) published two collections of poetry in the early 1970s, *The Hand That Cradles the Rock* (1971) and *Songs to a Handsome Woman* (1973). She is best known for her pioneering lesbian novel *Rubyfruit Jungle* (1973). A prolific novelist, she is the author of the Mrs. Murphy mystery series, as well as screenplays, teleplays, *Starting from Scratch: A Different Kind of Writer's Manual* (1988), and the memoir *Rita Will* (1997).

JAN CLAUSEN (b. 1950) was born in North Bend, Oregon, and educated at Reed College and the New School for Social Research, where she has taught since 1989. She has published two novels, a collection of short fiction, a memoir, essays and nonfiction including *A Movement of Poets: Thoughts on Poetry and Feminism* (1982), *Books and Life* (1989), and *Beyond Gay or Straight: Understanding Sexual Orientation* (1996); and several books of poetry: *After Touch* (1975), *Waking at the Bottom of the Dark* (1979), *Duration* (1983), *If You Like Difficulty* (2007), and *From a Glass House* (2007).

MICHELLE CLIFF (b. 1946) was born in Kingston, Jamaica, raised in Jamaica and New York City, and educated as an art historian at the Warburg Institute in London, where she specialized in the Italian Renaissance. After publishing a first book of poems, *Claiming an Identity They Taught Me To Despise* (1980), she wrote the novels *Abeng* (1984), *No Telephone to Heaven* (1987), and *Free Enterprise* (1993), two short story collections, and most recently a book of essays, *If I Could Write This in Fire* (2008).

LUCILLE CLIFTON (b. 1936) attended Howard University and graduated from Fredonia State Teachers College in Fredonia, New York. Submitted by Robert Hayden, her first collection, *Good Times* (1969), was published as the winner of the YW-YMHA Poetry Center's Discovery Award. She accepted the first of several writer-in-residence posts in 1971 when she began teaching at Coppin State University; she served as Maryland's Poet Laureate from 1979 to 1985. Her books include

Good News About the Earth (1972), *An Ordinary Woman* (1974), *Good Woman: Poems and a Memoir: 1969–1980* (1987), *Quilting: Poems 1987–1990* (1991), and *Blessing the Boats: New and Collected Poems 1988–2000* (2000), which won the National Book Award. She is also the author of more than 20 books for children. In 2007 she received the Ruth Lilly Poetry Prize, a lifetime achievement award from The Poetry Foundation.

JANE COOPER (1924–2007) was the author of *The Flashboat: Poems Collected and Reclaimed* (1999); her other books include *The Weather of Six Mornings* (1969), *Maps and Windows* (1974), *Scaffolding: New and Selected Poems* (1984), and *Green Notebook, Winter Road* (1994). She taught in the writing program at Sarah Lawrence College for almost four decades (1950–87), and also served as New York's State Poet (1995–97).

MARTHA COURTOT (1941–2000) grew up in a working-class Catholic family in Cincinnati, moved to New York in 1960, and later relocated to California, where she published two books of poetry, *Tribe* (1977) and *Journey* (1977), and contributed to lesbian-feminist periodicals. She was a member of Fat Chance, a Bay Area dance/performance troupe, from 1979 to 1981. Her later poems were collected posthumously in *The Bird Escapes* (2001).

BEVERLY DAHLEN (b. 1934) recently retired from a career as a creative writing and adult literacy teacher in the Bay Area. She studied poetry at California State in San Francisco, and published her first book, *Out of the Third*, in 1974. Beginning in 1983, she served as contributing editor for the magazine *HOW(ever)*. Sections of her serial poem *A Reading* have been brought out in several volumes since 1985; the most recent is *A Reading 18–20* (2006).

TOI DERRICOTTE (b. 1941) was born in Hamtramck, Michigan, and educated at Wayne State and New York University. She has taught at the University of Pittsburgh, where she is now professor of English, since 1991. In 1996, with Cornelius Eady, she founded Cave Canem, a summer retreat and support organization for African-American poets. She has published four books of poetry—*The Empress of the Death House* (1978), *Natural Birth* (1983), *Captivity* (1989), and *Tender* (1997)—and a memoir, *The Black Notebooks* (1997). Among other honors, she has won the Lucille Medwick Memorial Award from the Poetry Society of America (1985), National Endowment for the Arts fellowships in 1985 and 1990, and the Pushcart Prize in 1989.

DIANE DI PRIMA (b. 1934) was affiliated with the Beat poets in the 1950s. In 1958 she published her first collection, *This Kind of Bird Flies Backward* (1958), with Totem Press, a small press founded by LeRoi Jones (later Amiri Baraka), with whom she later collaborated on *The Floating Bear*, a literary magazine. She was co-founder and director of the Poets Theatre in New York City and the Poets Press. After moving from New York to northern California she helped establish, with Robert Duncan and David Meltzer, a Masters in Poetics program at the New College of California; she was co-founder and a teacher at the San Francisco Institute of Magical and Healing Arts. Her most ambitious work is the serial poem *Loba*, which she began working on in the early 1970s. The author of more than 40 books, her recent collections include *The Ones I Used To Laugh With* (2003), and *TimeBomb* (2006). In addition to her poetry, she is the author of *Memoirs of a Beatnik* (1969) and other novels, the plays collected in *Zip Code* (1994), a short story collection, and the memoir *Recollections of My Life As a Woman: The New York Years* (2001). She has also exhibited her work as a photographer, collagist, and watercolorist.

RACHEL BLAU DUPLESSIS (b. 1941) has had a distinguished career not only as a poet but as a literary critic and essayist, whose works include *Writing Beyond the Ending: Narrative Strategies of Twentieth-Century Women Writers* (1985), *H.D.: The Career of That Struggle* (1986), *The Pink Guitar: Writing as Feminist Practice* (1990), *Genders, Races, and Religious Cultures in Modern American Poetry, 1908–1934* (2001), and *Blue Studios: Poetry and Its Cultural Work* (2006). She has taught English at Temple University since 1974. Among her poetry collections are *Wells* (1980), *Gypsy / Moth* (1984), *Tabula Rosa* (1987), *Draft X: Letters* (1991), *Drafts 3–14* (1991), *Drafts 15–XXX* (1997), *Drafts 1–38, Toll* (2001), *Drafts 39–57, Pledge, with Draft, Unnumbered: Précis* (2004), and *Torques, Drafts 58–76* (2007).

CAROLYN FORCHÉ (b. 1950) won the Yale Younger Poets award for her first book of poems, *Gathering the Tribes* (1976). She worked as a journalist and human rights activist in El Salvador from 1978 to 1980, editing *Women and War in El Salvador* (1980) and publishing *Flowers from the Volcano* (1982), a translation of poems by the Salvadoran-exiled Nicaraguan writer Claribel Alegría. Her later books of poetry include *The Country Between Us* (1981, winner of the Academy of American Poets' Lamont Poetry Prize), *The Angel of History* (1994), and *Blue Hour* (2002). In 1998 she received the Edita and Ira Morris Hiroshima Foundation Award for Peace and Culture in Stockholm in recognition of her work for human rights. She also edited the anthology *Against Forgetting: Twentieth-Century Poetry of Witness* (1993). Born in Detroit, she is currently Lannan Visiting Professor of Poetry at Georgetown University.

KATHLEEN FRASER (b. 1937) received the YW-YMHA Poetry Center's Discovery Award and the New School's Frank O'Hara Poetry Prize in 1964. She has published almost 20 collections of poetry, including *What I Want* (1974), *Magritte Series* (1977), *New Shoes* (1978), *Notes Preceding Trust* (1987), *When New Time Folds Up* (1993) *WING* (1995), and *Discrete Categories Forced into Coupling* (2004). She has taught at the Iowa Writers' Workshop and the Naropa Institute; from 1972 to 1992 she was a professor of creative writing at San Francisco State University, where she directed the Poetry Center and established the American Poetry Archives. In 1983 she founded the journal *HOW(ever)*, which she edited until 1991. She is the editor of *Feminist Poetics: A Consideration of the Female Construction of Language* (1984).

ELSA GIDLOW (1898–1986) was born in Hull, England, and as a child immigrated with her family to Quebec. She worked as poetry editor for *Pearson's Magazine* in New York in the 1920s; her first collection of poems, *On a Grey Thread*, was published in 1923. Four years later she moved to northern California, where she lived for the rest of her life. In 1962, with Alan Watts, she co-founded the Society for Comparative Religion; she was also a founder of the Druid Heights Artists' Retreat in Mill Valley, California, and Druid Heights Books, a small press. Gidlow's later works include *Moods of Eros* (1970), *Makings for Meditation* (1973), *Ask No Man Pardon: The Philosophic Significance of Being Lesbian* (1975), and two volumes of *Sapphic Songs* (1976, 1982). Her autobiography, *Elsa: I Come with My Songs*, was published in 1986.

LOUISE GLÜCK (b. 1943) was raised on Long Island and is currently Rosencranz writer-in-residence at Yale. She served as U.S. Poet Laureate (2003–2004), and has won both the Pulitzer Prize for Poetry (for *The Wild Iris*, 1993), and the National Book Critics' Circle Award (for *Triumph of Achilles*, 1985). She has published many other poetry collections, including *Firstborn* (1968), *The House on Marshland* (1975), *The Garden* (1976), *Descending Figure* (1980), *Ararat* (1990), *The First Four Books of Poems* (1995), *Meadowlands* (1996), *Vita Nova* (1999), *The Seven Ages* (2001), *October* (2004), and *Averno* (2006), and a book of essays on poetry, *Proofs and Theories* (1994).

JORIE GRAHAM (b. 1950) was born in New York and educated at the Sorbonne, New York University, and the Iowa Writers' Workshop. She was a MacArthur Fellow in 1990, and has been Boylston Professor of Rhetoric and Oratory at Harvard since 1999. Her books include *Hybrids of Plants and Ghosts* (1980), *Erosion* (1983), *The End of Beauty* (1987), *Region of Unlikeness* (1991), *Materialism* (1993), *The Dream of the Unified Field: Poems, 1974–1994* (1995, winner of the Pulitzer Prize in Poetry), *The Errancy* (1997), *Swarm* (2000), *Never* (2002), *Overlord* (2005), and *Sea Change* (2008).

JUDY GRAHN (b. 1940) co-founded the Women's Press Collective in Oakland in 1969. The Collective published several of

Grahn's early books, including *Edward the Dyke* (1971), *The Common Woman* (1973), *A Woman Is Talking to Death* (1974), and *She Who* (1977). Her poems have since been gathered in *The Work of a Common Woman: The Collected Poetry of Judy Grahn, 1964–1977* (1978). She is also the author of *The Highest Apple: Sappho and the Lesbian Poetic Tradition* (1985), *Another Mother Tongue: Gay Words, Gay Worlds* (1990), *Blood, Bread, and Roses: How Menstruation Created the World* (1993), and the novel *Mundane's World* (1988).

SUSAN GRIFFIN (b. 1943) published her first book of poems, *Dear Sky*, with Shameless Hussy Press in 1971; her most recent is *Bending Home: Selected & New Poems, 1967–1998* (1998). Her play *Voices* was staged in 1974 and produced in a television adaptation, which won an Emmy. She has written about social, philosophical, and ecological concerns in *Woman and Nature: The Roaring Inside Her* (1978), *Rape: The Power of Consciousness* (1979), *Pornography and Silence* (1981), *A Chorus of Stones: The Private Life of War* (1992), *The Book of the Courtesans: A Catalogue of Their Virtues* (2001), and *Wrestling with the Angel of Democracy: On Being an American Citizen* (2008).

MARILYN HACKER (b. 1942) won the National Book Award for *Presentation Piece* (1974). Among her other volumes of poetry are *Assumptions* (1985), *Winter Numbers* (1994), *Squares and Courtyards* (2000), and *Desesperanto: Poems 1999–2002* (2003). She has been an editor of the science-fiction magazine *Quark*, *Thirteenth Moon*, *The Little Magazine*, and *The Kenyon Review*. Hacker has taught creative writing and French at several universities, and has published translations of French poets such as Claire Malroux, Marie Etienne, and Guy Goffette. She is a two-time winner of the Lambda Literary Award in Poetry, and in 1994 received the Poetry Society of America's John Masefield Memorial Prize for "Cancer Winter." She currently directs the M.A. program in creative writing at the City College of New York.

JANA HARRIS (b. 1947) has taught poetry at San Francisco State, the City University of New York, and the University of Washington, Seattle. Her books of poetry include *This House That Rocks with Every Truck on the Road* (1976), *Pin Money* (1977), *The Clackamas* (1980), *Who's That Pushy Bitch?* (1981), *Manhattan As a Second Language* (1982), *The Sourlands* (1989), *Oh How Can I Keep on Singing? Voices of Pioneer Women* (1993), *The Dust of Everyday Life: An Epic Poem of the Pacific Northwest* (1997), and *We Never Speak of It: Idaho-Wyoming Poems, 1889– 90* (2003). She has also written two novels, *Alaska* (1980) and *The Pearl of Ruby City* (1998).

FANNY HOWE (b. 1940) was born in Buffalo, New York, and now lives in Massachusetts; she recently retired from the University of California, San Diego, where she was Professor of Language and Literature and co-directed the M.F.A. program in writing. She has published many books of poetry, beginning with *Eggs* (1970) and recently including *Selected Poems* (2000, winner of the Lenore Marshall Poetry Prize), *On the Ground* (2005), and *The Lyrics* (2007). She is also the author of a collection of short stories, many novels, and the essay collections *The Wedding Dress: Meditations on Work and Life* (2000) and *The Winter Sun: Notes on a Vocation* (2009).

ERICA JONG (b. 1942) published her first collection, *Fruits & Vegetables*, in 1971, followed two years later by *Half Lives*. Her bestselling novel *Fear of Flying*, also published in 1973, was both celebrated and reviled for its candor about sexuality; it has been translated into more than 25 languages. Jong's other poetry collections are *Loveroot* (1975), *At the Edge of the Body* (1979), *Ordinary Miracles* (1983), and *Becoming Light* (1991). She has written the historical novels *Shylock's Daughter* (1987) and *Sappho's Leap* (2003) as well as *The Devil at Large* (1993), about Henry Miller, and memoirs such as *Fear of Fifty* (1994).

JUNE JORDAN (1936–2002) was born in Harlem and attended Barnard College and the University of Chicago, after which she worked as an assistant to documentary filmmaker Frederick

Wiseman and with R. Buckminster Fuller on housing designs for low-income families. Her first book, *Who Look at Me* (1969), completed a project originally begun by Langston Hughes. She went on to publish plays and libretti; poetry and fiction for children and young adults; a memoir, *Soldier: A Poet's Childhood* (1989); several essay collections including *Civil Wars: Selected Essays, 1963–80* (1981), *On Call: Political Essays, 1981–1985* (1985), and *Some of Us Did Not Die: New and Selected Essays* (2002); and many books of poetry. She was professor of Afro-American studies at Berkeley from 1989 until her death. *Directed by Desire: The Collected Poems of June Jordan* was published posthumously in 2005.

CAROLYN KIZER (b. 1925) is the author of eight volumes of poetry, including *Midnight Was My Cry: New and Selected Poems* (1971), *Harping On: Poems 1985–1995* (1996), and *Cool Calm & Collected* (2000), her collected poems. She has published translations and collections of critical essays as well as edited anthologies such as *100 Great Poems by Women* (1985). A founder and editor of *Poetry Northwest*, she served as the first Director of Literature Program for the National Endowment for the Arts and has taught at several universities. She has received the Frost Medal and the American Academy of Arts and Letters award in literature; *Yin: New Poems* (1984) was awarded the Pulitzer Prize.

IRENA KLEPFISZ (b. 1941) was born in the Warsaw Ghetto, where her father was killed resisting the Nazis in 1943. Klepfisz's mother was able to pass as a gentile Pole and spent the last years of the war in hiding in the Polish countryside with her daughter. They immigrated to Sweden in 1946 and then to the United States in 1949. Klepfisz's writings have been collected in *Different Enclosures: The Poetry and Prose of Irena Klepfisz* (1985), *A Few Words in the Mother Tongue: Poems Selected and New 1971–1990* (1990), and *Dreams of an Insomniac: Jewish Feminist Essays, Speeches, and Diatribes* (1990). She is also the co-editor of *The Tribe of Dina: A Jewish Women's Anthology* (1986). A founding editor of the magazine *Conditions*, she has taught at Michigan

State University and Barnard College; she was awarded a National Endowment for the Arts Fellowship in Poetry in 1988.

MAXINE KUMIN (b. 1925) is the author of 15 books of poetry, including the Pulitzer Prize–winning *Up Country: Poems of New England* (1972), *Our Ground Time Here Will Be Brief: New and Selected Poems* (1982), and, most recently, *Jack and Other New Poems* (2005). She has published more than 20 children's books, several novels and essay collections, and the memoir *Inside the Halo and Beyond: Anatomy of a Recovery* (2000), about a near-fatal horse-riding accident and its aftermath. She served as Poetry Consultant to the Library of Congress, 1981–82, and Poet Laureate of New Hampshire, 1989–94; among her many awards are the Poets' Prize (for *Looking for Luck*, 1992) and the Ruth Lilly Poetry Prize.

JOAN LARKIN (b. 1939) co-founded the lesbian feminist press Out & Out Books in 1975, and in the same year edited the groundbreaking *Amazon Poetry: An Anthology*, with Elly Bulkin. She has since edited other LGBT anthologies including *Lesbian Poetry* (1981), *Gay and Lesbian Poetry in Our Time* (1988, with Carl Morse; winner of the Lambda Literary Award), and *A Woman Like That: Lesbian and Bisexual Writers Tell Their Coming Out Stories* (1999), and she has published several collections of her own poetry: *Housework* (1975), *A Long Sound* (1986), *Cold River* (1997), and *My Body: New and Selected Poems* (2007). She was assistant professor of English at Brooklyn College of the City University of New York from 1969 until 1994, and continues to teach poetry in M.F.A. programs, including at Sarah Lawrence and Drew University.

DENISE LEVERTOV (1923–1997) was born in Ilford, Essex, and educated at home. She worked as a nurse in London hospitals during World War II, and immigrated to the U.S. in 1948, having already published a book of poems, *The Double Image* (1946). She went on to produce a large and various body of work in her adopted country, including poems, translations, essays, and memoirs. During the Vietnam War—against which she organized protests and engaged in civil disobedience—her writings became notably political. From 1981 until her death she was professor of English at Stanford. Her many other poetry books include *Here and Now* (1957), *Collected Earlier Poems, 1940–1960* (1979), *Poems, 1960–1967* (1983), *Poems, 1968–1972* (1987), and the posthumous *This Great Unknowing: Last Poems* (1999). She also published essay collections *The Poet in the World* (1973), *Light Up the Cave* (1981), *New & Selected Essays* (1992), and *Tesserae: Memories and Suppositions* (1995).

AUDRE LORDE (1934–1992) graduated from Hunter College in 1959 and received a degree in library science from Columbia in 1961; during the 1960s, she supported herself as a librarian while working as an activist and publishing poems in magazines and anthologies such as Langston Hughes' *New Negro Poets: USA* (1962). She was awarded a National Endowment for the Arts grant in 1968 and served as poet-in-residence at Tougaloo College in Mississippi, the first of several teaching appointments. Her first book, *The First Cities*, was brought out by Diane di Prima's Poets Press that same year. Collections that followed include *Cables to Rage* (1970), *Coal* (1976), *The Black Unicorn* (1978), *Our Dead Behind Us* (1986), and *Undersong: Chosen Poems Old and New* (1992). *The Collected Poems of Audre Lorde* was published posthumously in 1997. She was also the author of *The Cancer Journals* (1980), an account of her struggles with breast cancer. In the late 1980s she co-founded Kitchen Table: Women of Color Press; in 1991 she was honored as New York's Poet Laureate.

CYNTHIA MACDONALD (b. 1928) studied music at Mannes College after graduating from Bennington, and began her career as a concert and opera singer. Later turning to poetry, she published *Amputations* (1972), *(W)holes* (1980), *Living Wills* (1991), and *I Can't Remember* (1997). She taught creative writing at Sarah Lawrence, Johns Hopkins, and the University of Houston, where she co-founded the creative writing program and is now professor emerita. In 1986 she graduated from the

Houston-Galveston Psychoanalytic Institute, and afterward practiced as a psychoanalyst.

BERNADETTE MAYER (b. 1945) was born in Brooklyn and educated at the New School for Social Research. She achieved considerable notoriety as a performance artist for her 1972 exhibition *Memory*, which combined photographs and narration, and her writing often experiments with the boundaries between poetry and prose. Her early writings were collected in *A Bernadette Mayer Reader* (1992), and she has subsequently published *The Desire of Mothers to Please Others in Letters* (1994), *Proper Name and Other Stories* (1996), *Another Smashed Pinecone* (1998), *Two Haloed Mourners* (1998), and *Scarlet Tanager* (2005).

HONOR MOORE (b. 1945) was born in New York City, graduated from Radcliffe College, and attended the Yale School of Drama. She has taught at many institutions including New York University, the New School, and Columbia. Along with three collections of poetry—*Memoir* (1988), *Darling* (2001), and *Red Shoes* (2006)—she has written a play, *Mourning Pictures* (1974), which was produced on Broadway, a biography, *The White Blackbird: A Life of the Painter Margarett Sargent by Her Granddaughter* (1996), and most recently *The Bishop's Daughter: A Memoir* (2008). Along with the present volume, she has edited *The New Women's Theatre: Ten Plays by Contemporary American Women* (1977), *Amy Lowell: Selected Poems* (2004), and *The Stray Dog Cabaret: A Book of Russian Poems*, translated by Paul Schmidt (2006).

CAROL MUSKE-DUKES (b. 1945) founded Free Space, a creative writing program at the Women's House of Detention on Rikers Island, New York, in 1972, and directed the program for a decade. She has since taught creative writing at the University of Southern California, Los Angeles, where she is now professor of English. Under her maiden name she published *Camouflage* (1975), *Skylight* (1981), *Wyndmere* (1985), *Applause* (1989), *Red Trousseau* (1993), and *An Octave above Thunder* (1997), all collections of poetry; she is also the author, as Carol Muske-

Dukes, of the novels *Dear Digby* (1989), *Saving St. Germ* (1993), *Life after Death* (2001), and *Channeling Mark Twain* (2008); a book of literary criticism, *Women and Poetry: Truth, Autobiography, and the Shape of the Self* (1997); an essay collection, *Married to the Icepick Killer: A Poet in Hollywood* (2002); and her most recent collection of poems, *Sparrow* (2004). In 1997 she received the Witter Bynner Award from the Library of Congress, and in 2008 she was appointed Poet Laureate of California.

JANE MILLER (b. 1949) is the author of *Many Junipers, Heartbeats* (1980), *Black Holes, Black Stockings* (1983, with Olga Broumas), *American Odalisque* (1987), *August Zero* (1993), *Memory at These Speeds: New and Selected Poems* (1996), *Wherever You Lay Your Head* (1999), and *A Palace of Pearls* (2005), along with a collection of criticism, *Working Time: Essays on Poetry, Culture, and Travel* (1990). A native of New York City, she teaches creative writing at the University of Arizona, Tucson.

ROBIN MORGAN (b. 1941) edited the groundbreaking anthologies *Sisterhood Is Powerful* (1970) and *Sisterhood Is Global* (1984) and served as editor-in-chief of *Ms.* magazine from 1989 to 1993. She was a leading organizer of the 1968 Atlantic City protests against the Miss America pageant and a founding member of many activist groups including Women's International Terrorist Conspiracy from Hell (WITCH), Women Against Pornography, and the Feminist Writers' Guild. Her poetry collections include *Upstairs in the Garden: Selected and New Poems* (1994) and *A Hot January: Poems 1996–1999* (1999). She is the author of the novels *Dry Your Smile* (1987) and *The Burning Time* (2006), and other works such as *Going Too Far: The Personal Chronicle of a Feminist* (1974), *The Demon Lover: The Roots of Terrorism* (1989), and *Fighting Words: A Toolkit for Combating the Religious Right* (2006).

EILEEN MYLES (b. 1949) graduated from the University of Massachusetts and then moved to New York City. She studied at St. Mark's Poetry Project, serving as its artistic director from 1984 to 1986, and has taught at a number of colleges and universities, most recently directing the writing program at the University of California, San Diego (2002–2007). She gave her first poetry reading in 1974 at CBGB, and has since won a reputation as a performer of her own work. In print her poetry has appeared as *The Irony of the Leash* (1978), *A Fresh Young Voice from the Plains* (1981), *Sappho's Boat* (1982), *1969* (1989), *Not Me* (1991), *Maxfield Parrish* (1995), *School of Fish* (1997), *Skies* (2001), and *Sorry, Tree* (2007). She has also published plays, short-story collections *Bread and Water* (1987) and *Chelsea Girls* (1994), a novel, *Cool for You* (2000), and *The Importance of Being Iceland: Travel Essays on Art* (2009).

ALICE NOTLEY (b. 1945) graduated from Barnard College and the Iowa Writers' Workshop. She married poet Ted Berrigan in 1972, and the two associated with other writers of the New York School; Berrigan died in 1983, and in 2005, with their two sons, she edited *The Collected Poems of Ted Berrigan*. She has published many volumes of her own poetry, beginning with *165 Meeting House Lane* (1971), and including more recently *Disobedience* (2001, recipient of the Griffin Prize), *From the Beginning* (2004), *Grave of Light: Selected Poems, 1970–2000* (2006), and *Alma; or The Dead Women* (2006). In 2005, the University of Michigan Press collected her literary criticism as *Coming After: Essays on Poetry*.

SHARON OLDS (b. 1942) was born in San Francisco and educated at Stanford and Columbia; she has taught creative writing at New York University since 1990. Her book *The Dead and the Living* (1984) won the National Book Critics Circle award and the Lamont Poetry Prize. She is also the author of *Satan Says* (1980), *The Gold Cell* (1987), *The Matter of This World* (1987), *The Sign of Saturn* (1991), *The Father* (1992), *The Wellspring* (1995), *Blood, Tin, Straw* (1999), and *The Unswept Room* (2002). From 1998 to 2000 she served as New York State Poet.

ALICIA OSTRIKER (b. 1937) is the author of *Songs* (1969), *A Woman Under the Surface* (1982), *The Crack in Everything* (1996), *The Little Space* (1998), *No Heaven* (2005), and many other volumes of poetry. As a critic she has published widely on contemporary women's poetry and religion in books such as *Stealing the Language: The Emergence of Women Poets in America* (1986), *Feminist Revision and the Bible* (1992), *The Nakedness of the Fathers: Biblical Visions and Revisions* (1994), and *For the Love of God: The Bible as an Open Book* (2007). She taught English and creative writing for more than four decades at Rutgers University, where she was named professor emerita in 2004.

MAUREEN OWEN (b. 1943) has collected her poems in *Country Rush* (1973), *No Travels Journal* (1975), *Hearts in Space* (1980), *AE (Amelia Earhart)* (1984), *Zombie Notes* (1985), *Imaginary Income* (1992), *Untapped Maps* (1993), *American Rush* (1998), and *Erosion's Pull* (2006). She has been an adjunct professor at Naropa University in Boulder, Colorado, since 2003.

PAT PARKER (1944–1989) is the author of *Child of Myself* (1972), *Pit Stop: Words* (1974), *Movement in Black: The Collected Poetry of Pat Parker, 1961–1978* (1978, expanded edition, 1999), *Womanslaughter* (1978), and *Jonestown and Other Madness* (1985). A lifelong activist, she founded the Black Women's Revolutionary Council in 1980 and served as director of the Feminist Women's Health Center in Oakland, California.

MOLLY PEACOCK (b. 1947) has written many books of poetry including *And Live Apart* (1980), *Raw Heaven* (1984), *Take Heart* (1989), *Original Love* (1995), *Understory* (1996), *Cornucopia: New and Selected Poems, 1975–2002* (2002), and *The Second Blush* (2008), as well as a memoir, *Paradise, Piece by Piece* (1998). Born in Buffalo, New York, she studied poetry at SUNY-Binghamton and The Writing Seminars at Johns Hopkins. A former president of the Poetry Society of America and co-creator of the "Poetry in Motion" project to include poems in subways and buses, she has also performed in *The Shimmering Verge*, a one-woman show in poems, in London and throughout the U.S. and Canada. She now lives in Toronto.

MARGE PIERCY (b. 1936) was an activist in the civil rights movement and Students for a Democratic Society in the 1960s.

She published her first book, the poetry collection *Breaking Camp*, in 1968, followed the next year by *Hard Loving* and the novel *Going Down Fast*. A prolific novelist and poet, she has written more than 35 books, among them the poetry volumes *The Moon Is Always Female* (1980) and *What Are Big Girls Made Of?* (1997) and the novels *Small Changes* (1973), *Woman on the Edge of Time* (1976), and *Sex Wars* (2005).

SYLVIA PLATH (1932–1963) attended Smith College and studied at Cambridge University on a Fulbright Fellowship. While in England she met the poet Ted Hughes, whom she married in 1956; the couple lived in Boston while Plath taught at Smith, then settled in England. *The Colossus and Other Poems* was published in Britain in 1960 and in the U.S. two years later. The BBC broadcast her radio play *Three Women: A Monologue for Three Voices* in 1962. She separated from Hughes in fall 1962 and lived with their two children in London through the winter, writing the poems that would appear in *Ariel* (1965), published in a version edited by Hughes after Plath's suicide on February 11, 1963. Her other works include the autobiographical novel *The Bell Jar*, first published under a pseudonym in 1963; *Crossing the Water: Transitional Poems* (1971), *Winter Trees* (1972), *Letters Home: Correspondence, 1950–1963* (1975), *The Collected Poems* (1981), *The Unabridged Journals of Sylvia Plath* (2000), and *Ariel: The Restored Edition* (2004).

KATHA POLLITT (b. 1949), longtime columnist and editor for *The Nation*, has collected her essays and journalism in *Reasonable Creatures: Essays on Women and Feminism* (1994), *Subject to Debate: Sense and Dissents on Women, Politics, and Culture* (2001), *Virginity or Death! And Other Social and Political Issues of Our Time* (2006), and *Learning to Drive, and Other Life Stories* (2007). She won the National Book Critics Circle Award for her poetry collection *Antarctic Traveler* (1982); her most recent is *The Mind-Body Problem* (2009).

MARIE PONSOT (b. 1921) was raised in Queens, New York, and studied 17th-century literature at Columbia University.

She lived in Paris for three years after World War II, marrying painter Claude Ponsot, with whom she had seven children. She has worked as a freelance radio and television writer, as a translator of French children's books, and as a literature professor. Her books of poetry include *True Minds* (1956), *Admit Impediment* (1981), *The Green Dark* (1988), *The Bird Catcher* (1998; winner of the National Book Critics Circle Award), and *Springing: New and Selected Poems* (2002). She is also the author, with Rosemary Deen, of two books about literary composition: *Beat Not the Poor Desk* (1982) and *The Common Sense* (1985).

ADRIENNE RICH (b. 1929) graduated from Radcliffe College in 1951, the year her collection *A Change of World* was selected for publication in the Yale Series of Younger Poets. Over the following decades her work became more radical formally and in terms of its political engagement. When Rich won the National Book Award for *Diving into the Wreck* (1973), she shared it with her fellow nominees Alice Walker and Audre Lorde on behalf of all women who are silenced. Her many volumes of poetry include *The Dream of a Common Language* (1978), *The Fact of a Doorframe: Poems Selected and New 1950–1984* (1984; expanded edition, 2002), *An Atlas of the Difficult World: Poems 1988–1991* (1991), *Dark Fields of the Republic: Poems 1991–1995* (1995), *Fox: Poems 1998–2000* (2001), *The School Among the Ruins: Poems 2000–2004* (2004), and *The Telephone Ringing in the Labyrinth: Poems 2004–2006* (2007); she is also the author of *Of Woman Born: Motherhood as Experience and Institution* (1986), *What Is Found There: Notebooks on Poetry and Politics* (1993), and several collections of essays. Her numerous honors include the Bollingen Prize, the Lannan Lifetime Achievement Award, the Ruth Lilly Poetry Prize, and a MacArthur Fellowship; in 1997, she refused to accept the National Medal of Arts, writing in explanation that "a President cannot meaningfully honor certain token artists while the people at large are so dishonored."

MURIEL RUKEYSER (1913–1980) published her first book, *Theory of Flight* (1935), in the Yale Series of Younger Poets. In addition to several collections of poetry, she also wrote biographies (of Willard Gibbs and Wendell Willkie), translations (of Octavio Paz and Gunnar Ekelöf, among others), the critical study *The Life of Poetry* (1949), and the novel *The Orgy* (1965). Among the many prizes awarded her were the Levinson Prize and the Shelley Memorial Award. Rukeyser's *Collected Poems* was published in 1979; in 2004, Adrienne Rich edited her *Selected Poems* for The Library of America's American Poets Project series.

SONIA SANCHEZ (b. 1934) emerged as a member of the Black Arts movement. One of the "Broadside Quartet" of activist poets (with Nikki Giovanni, Etheridge Knight, and Don L. Lee [later Haki Madhubuti]), she published her debut book, *Home Coming*, in 1969. Subsequent works include *We a BaddDDD People* (1970), *Liberation Poems* (1971), *I've Been a Woman: New and Selected Poems* (1981), *Homegirls and Handgrenades* (1985), *Shake Loose My Skin: New and Selected Poems* (1999), and the spoken-word album *Full Moon of Sonia* (2004). As a playwright she is the author of *The Bronx Is Next* (1968), *Sister Sonji* (1970), *I'm Black When I'm Singing, I'm Blue When I Ain't* (1982), and other plays. She taught English and Women's Studies at Temple University from 1977 until her retirement in 1999.

ANNE SEXTON (1928–1974) began writing her mature poems in the late 1950s, after repeated bouts of depression, an attempted suicide, and hospitalization at the Westwood Lodge, a psychiatric facility in Weymouth, Massachusetts. She enrolled in a poetry workshop in 1957, where she met lifelong friend Maxine Kumin, and audited a class taught by Robert Lowell at Boston University, in which one of her classmates was Sylvia Plath. Her first book, *To Bedlam and Part Way Back* (1960), was widely reviewed; her subsequent volumes include *All My Pretty Ones* (1962) and the Pulitzer Prize–winning *Live or Die* (1966). She committed suicide in 1974. *Words for Dr. Y.: Uncollected Poems* (1978), *Anne Sexton: A Self-Portrait in Letters* (1977), and an edition of *The Complete Poems* (1981) were published after her death.

MAY SWENSON (1913–1989) moved from her native Utah to New York City in 1936 and worked for the Federal Writers' Project. Her first book, *A Cage of Spines*, was published in 1958, and she worked as an editor at New Directions from 1959 to 1966. Her books include *To Mix With Time* (1963), the collection of shaped poems *Iconographs* (1970), *New and Selected Things Taking Place* (1978), and *In Other Words* (1987). She published poetry for children in *Poems to Solve* (1966) and *More Poems to Solve* (1971) and translated Swedish poets such as Tomas Transt.römer. She was awarded the Bollingen Prize in 1981 and a MacArthur Fellowship in 1987.

JEAN VALENTINE (b. 1943) won the Yale Younger Poets Award in 1965 for her collection *Dream Barker*. Her other volumes include *Pilgrims* (1969), *Growing Darkness, Growing Light* (1997), and *Little Boat* (2007). *Door in the Mountain: New and Collected Poems* (2004) received the National Book Award. She has taught creative writing at Sarah Lawrence College, New York University, and workshops at the 92nd Street Y in Manhattan.

DIANE WAKOSKI (b. 1937) studied with poets Josephine Miles and Thom Gunn at Berkeley. In 1960 she moved to New York City, where she worked as a junior high school teacher; her first collection, *Coins and Coffins*, was published in 1962. Among her later books of poetry are *The Collected Greed, Parts 1–13* (1984), *Emerald Ice: Selected Poems 1962–1987* (1988), *Argonaut Rose* (1998), and *The Butcher's Apron: New & Selected Poems* (2000). Her essays have been gathered in books such as *Variations on a Theme* (1976) and *Toward a New Poetry* (1979). Since the mid-1970s she has been writer-in-residence at Michigan State University.

ANNE WALDMAN (b. 1945) was raised in Greenwich Village, and after graduating from Bennington College returned to direct the St. Mark's Poetry Project, where she edited its literary magazine *The World*. In 1974, with Allen Ginsberg, she cofounded the Jack Kerouac School of Disembodied Poetics at the Naropa Institute. She has published many books of poetry, beginning with *On the Wing* (1968) and recently including *Marriage: A Sentence* (2000), *Structure of the World Compared to a Bubble* (2004), and *In the Room of Never Grieve: New and Selected Poems, 1985–2003* (2008).

ALICE WALKER (b. 1944) attended Spelman College and graduated from Sarah Lawrence College in 1965. As a civil-rights worker she registered voters in Georgia and taught in a Head Start program in Mississippi. Her first volume of poetry, *Once*, was published in 1968, followed by *Revolutionary Petunias* in 1973. Her efforts championing the work of Zora Neale Hurston were crucial to Hurston's rediscovery in the mid-1970s. Walker's novel *The Color Purple* (1982), winner of the Pulitzer Prize and the National Book Award, was an international bestseller, and inspired film (1985) and Broadway musical (2005) adaptations. Her poems have been gathered in *Her Blue Body Everything We Know: Earthling Poems, 1965–1990 Complete* (1991) and *Collected Poems* (2005). Among her other books are the novels *The Temple of My Familiar* (1989) and *Possessing the Secret of Joy* (1992), and *Now Is the Time To Open Your Heart* (2004), as well as *In Search of Our Mothers' Gardens: Womanist Prose* (1983) and *Living by the Word* (1988).

FRAN WINANT (b. 1943) was an activist in the post-Stonewall lesbian and gay rights movement, helping to found the Gay Liberation Front, the Radicalesbians, and a nonprofit food co-op, the Lesbian Food Conspiracy. With her partner Judy Grepperd, she also established the Violet Press, which published her collections *Looking at Women* (1971), *Dyke Jacket* (1976), *Goddess of Lesbian Dreams* (1980), and the anthology *We Are All Lesbians* (1975). She graduated from Fordham University in 1975 with an art degree. Her paintings have appeared in many exhibitions including the New Museum's 1982 "Extended Sensibilities: Homosexual Presence in Contemporary Art."

SOURCES AND ACKNOWLEDGMENTS

The poems in this volume are arranged by the approximate date of composition of the earliest poem included for each poet. Texts have mainly been taken from the first book edition in which each poem appeared, though in some cases subsequent editions of a poet's work have been preferred, and in other cases poems have been reprinted from anthologies.

The following list identifies the source for each of the poems included in this volume and provides copyright information and acknowledgments. Great care has been taken to trace all owners of copyrighted material included in this book. If any has inadvertently been omitted, acknowledgment will gladly be made in future printings.

alta, Miscarriage; 10 commandments for liberation: *Burn This and Memorize Yourself: Poems for Women* (New York: Times Change Press, 1971). Euridice: *I Am Not a Practicing Angel* (Trumansburg, New York: Crossing Press, 1975). Copyright © by Alta Gerrey. Reprinted by permission of the author.

Rae Armantrout, Anti-Short Story; Tone: *In the American Tree*, Ron Silliman, ed. (Orono, Maine: National Poetry Foundation, 1986). Copyright © 2001 by Rae Armantrout. Reprinted by permission of Wesleyan University Press.

Olga Broumas, Caritas: *Caritas* (Eugene: Jackrabbit Press, 1976). Copyright © 1999 by Olga Broumas. Reprinted with the permission of Copper Canyon Press, www.coppercanyonpress.org.

Rita Mae Brown, Sappho's Reply: *The Hand That Cradles the Rock* (Oakland: Diana Press, 1974). First published by New York University Press. Copyright © 1971 by Rita Mae Brown. Reprinted by permission of the Wendy Weil Agency, Inc.

Jan Clausen, After Touch: *After Touch* (Brooklyn: Out & Out Books, 1975). Copyright © 1975 by Jan Clausen. Reprinted by permission of the author.

Michelle Cliff, Women's Work: *Claiming an Identity They Taught Me To Despise* (Watertown, Massachusetts: Persephone Press, 1980). Copyright © 1980 by Michelle Cliff. Reprinted by permission of the author.

Lucille Clifton, miss rosie; the lost baby poem: *Good Woman: Poems and a Memoir* (Brockport: BOA Editions, 1987). Copyright © 1987 by Lucille Clifton. Reprinted with the permission of BOA Editions, Ltd., www.boaeditions.org.

Jane Cooper, The Green Notebook: *Green Notebook, Winter Road* (Gardiner, Maine: Tilbury House, 1994). Copyright © 1994 by Jane Cooper. Used by permission of W.W. Norton & Company, Inc.

Martha Courtot, i am a woman in ice: *Amazon Poetry: An Anthology of Lesbian Poetry*, Elly Bulkin & Joan Larkin, eds. (Brooklyn: Out & Out Books, 1975). Copyright © Martha Courtot.

Beverly Dahlen, Gesture: *Out of the Third* (San Francisco: Momo's Press, 1974). Copyright © 1974 by Beverly Dahlen. Reprinted by permission of the author.

Toi Derricotte, in knowledge of young boys: *Natural Birth* (Trumansburg, New York: Crossing Press, 1983). Copyright © 1983 by Toi Derricotte. Reprinted by permission of the author.

Diane Di Prima, Annunciation: *Loba* (New York: Penguin, 1998). Copyright © 1973, 1976, 1977, 1978, 1998 by Diane Di Prima. Used by permission of Penguin, a division of Penugin Group (USA) Inc.

Rachel Blau DuPlessis, Nessie: *Wells* (New York: Montemora Foundation, 1980). Copyright © 1980 by Rachel Blau DuPlessis. Reprinted by permission of the author.

Carolyn Forché, Burning the Tomato Worms: *Gathering the Tribes* (New Haven: Yale University Press, 1976). Copyright © 1976 by Carolyn Forché. Reprinted by permission of Yale University Press.

Kathleen Fraser, The History of My Feeling: *What I Want* (New York: Harper & Row, 1974). Copyright © 1997 by Kathleen Fraser. Reprinted by permission of Wesleyan University Press.

Elsa Gidlow, You say I am mysterious: *Makings for Meditation: A Collection of Parapoems, Reverant & Irreverant* (Mill Valley, California: Druid Heights Books, 1973). Copyright © Elsa Gidlow.

Louise Glück, Pomegranate; Dedication to Hunger: *The First Four Books of Poems* (Hopewell, New Jersey: Ecco Press, 1995). Copyright © 1971, 1972, 1973, 1974, 1975, 1976, 1977, 1978, 1979, 1980, 1985, 1995 by Louise Glück. Reprinted by permission of HarperCollins Publishers.

Jorie Graham, San Sepolcro: *The Dream of the Unified Field: Selected Poems, 1974–1994* (Hopewell, New Jersey: The Ecco Press, 1995). Copyright © 1995 by Jorie Graham. Reprinted by permission of HarperCollins Publishers.

Judy Grahn, A Woman Is Talking to Death: *The Work of a Common Woman: The Collected Poetry of Judy Grahn, 1964-1977* (New York: St. Martin's Press, 1978). "A Woman Is Talking to Death" was originally published by The Oakland Women's Press Collective (1974) and is forthcoming in a collection from Aunt Lute Press in San Francisco (Spring 2009). Copyright © 1974 by Judy Grahn. Reprinted by permission of the author.

Susan Griffin, I Like to Think of Harriet Tubman; Three Poems for Women; An Answer to a Man's Question, "What Can I Do About Women's Liberation?": *Like the Iris of An Eye* (New York: Harper & Row, 1976). Copyright © by Susan Griffin. Reprinted by permission of the author.

Marilyn Hacker, Elegy: *Presentation Piece* (New York: Viking Press, 1974). Copyright © 1974 by Marilyn Hacker. Used by permission of W.W. Norton & Company, Inc.

Jana Harris, Don't Cheapen Yourself: *Pin Money* (Fairfax, CA: Jungle Garden Press, 1976). Copyright © 1976 by Jana Harris. Reprinted by permission of the author. First published in *Ms.* magazine.

Fanny Howe, The Nursery: *Selected Poems* (Berkeley: University of California Press, 2000). Copyright © 2000 by Fanny Howe. Reprinted by permission of the University of California Press.

Erica Jong, Why I Died: *Half-Lives* (New York: Holt, Rinehart and Winston, 1973). Copyright © 1973 by Erica Mann Jong. Reprinted by permission of the author.

June Jordan, Poem: On Declining Values; Roman Poem Number Six: *New Days: Poems of Exile and Return* (New York: Emerson Hall, 1974). Case in Point: *Directed by Desire: The Collected Poems of June Jordan*

Marge Piercy, The nuisance: *To Be of Use* (Garden City: Doubleday, 1973). Rape Poem: *Living in the Open* (New York: Alfred A. Knopf, 1976). Copyright © 1982 by Marge Piercy. Used by permission of Alfred A. Knopf, a division of Random House, Inc.

Sylvia Plath, The Applicant: *The Collected Poems* (New York: Harper & Row, 1981). Copyright © 1963 by Ted Hughes. Reprinted by permission of HarperCollins Publishers.

Katha Pollitt, Metaphors of Women: *Atlantic Traveller* (New York: Alfred A. Knopf, 1981). Copyright © 1981 by Katha Pollitt. Used by permission of Alfred A. Knopf, a division of Random House, Inc.

Marie Ponsot, Among Women: *Admit Impediment* (New York: Alfred A. Knopf, 1981). Copyright © 1958, 1960, 1964, 1977, 1979, 1980, 1981 by Marie Ponsot. Used by permission of Alfred A. Knopf, a division of Random House, Inc.

Adrienne Rich, Planetarium: *The Will To Change: Poems 1968–1970* (New York: W.W. Norton, 1971). Diving into the Wreck: *Diving into the Wreck* (New York: W.W. Norton, 1973). Phantasia for Elvira Shatayev: *The Dream of a Common Language: Poems 1974–1977* (New York: W.W. Norton, 1978). Copyright © 1973, 1978 by W.W. Norton & Company, Inc. Used by permission of the author and W.W. Norton & Company, Inc.

Muriel Rukeyser, Käthe Kollwitz; Not To Be Printed, Not To Be Said, Not To Be Thought: *The Collected Poems of Muriel Rukeyser*, Janet E. Kaufman, Anne F. Herzog, Jan Heller Levi, eds. (Pittsburgh: University of Pittsburgh Press, 2005). Copyright © 1968, 1976 by Muriel Rukeyser. Reprinted by permission of International Creative Management, Inc.

Sonia Sanchez, personal letter no. 2: *Home Coming* (Detroit: Broadside Press, 1969). Copyright © 1969 by Sonia Sanchez. Reprinted by permission of the author. a poem for my father: *We a BaddDDD People* (Detroit: Broadside Press, 1970). Copyright © 1970 by Sonia Sanchez. Reprinted by permission of the author.

Anne Sexton, The Ballad of the Lonely Masturbator: *The Complete Poems* (New York: Houghton Mifflin, 1981). Copyright © 1967, 1968, 1969 by Anne Sexton. Reprinted by permission of Houghton Mifflin Harcourt Publishing Company. All rights reserved.

May Swenson, O'Keeffe Retrospective: *New & Selected Things Taking Place* (Boston: Little, Brown, 1978). Copyright © 1978. Reprinted with permission of The Literary Estate of May Swenson.

Jean Valentine. Susan's Photograph: *Door in the Mountain: New and Collected Poems, 1965–2003* (Middletown, Connecticut: Wesleyan Uni-

This volume presents the texts of the editions chosen for inclusion here, but it does not attempt to reproduce nontextual features of their typographic design. The texts are presented without change, except for the correction of typographical errors, cited by page and line number: 88.12, top a; 89.15 indency; 89.17; ommission; 92.21, care; 121.8, Signor; 154.10, O'Keefe; 154.29, cillia; 154.30, satelite; 156.8, mantila; 164.4, Anderson; 165.9, Twin; 166.7 Allen; 166.13, Guinivere; 169.6, Goodbye [no closing quote]; 170.11, sandles; 200.18, Heineckens; 200.13, Barbara. [no closing quote].

INDEX OF POETS, TITLES, AND FIRST LINES

AMERICAN POETS PROJECT